The Hazeley Family

THE SCHOMBURG LIBRARY OF
NINETEENTH-CENTURY BLACK WOMEN WRITERS

General Editor, Henry Louis Gates, Jr.

Titles are listed chronologically; collections that include works published over a
span of years are listed according to the publication date of their initial work.

The Hazeley Family

MRS. A. E. JOHNSON

With an Introduction by
BARBARA CHRISTIAN

❧ ❧ ❧

❧ ❧ ❧

New York   Oxford
OXFORD UNIVERSITY PRESS
1988

Oxford University Press

Oxford   New York   Toronto
Delhi   Bombay   Calcutta   Madras   Karachi
Petaling Jaya   Singapore   Hong Kong   Tokyo
Nairobi   Dar Es Salaam   Cape Town
Melbourne   Auckland

and associated companies in
Beirut   Berlin   Ibadan   Nicosia

Copyright © 1988 by Oxford University Press, Inc.

Published by Oxford University Press, Inc.,
200 Madison Avenue, New York, New York 10016

Library of Congress Cataloging-in-Publication Data

Johnson, A. E. (Amelia E.), b. 1859.
The Hazeley family.
(The Schomburg library of nineteenth-century black
women writers)
I. Title.   II. Series.
PS2134.J515H39   1988   813'.4   87-28258
ISBN 0-19-50525
ISBN 0-19-50525

2 4 6 8 10 9 7 5 3 1

Printed in the United States of America
on acid-free paper

The
Schomburg Library
of
Nineteenth-Century
Black Women Writers
is
Dedicated
in Memory
of

PAULINE AUGUSTA COLEMAN GATES

1916–1987

PUBLISHER'S NOTE

Whenever possible, the volumes in this set were reproduced directly from original materials. When availability, physical condition of original texts, or other circumstances prohibited this, volumes or portions of volumes were reset.

FOREWORD
In Her Own Write

Henry Louis Gates, Jr.

One muffled strain in the Silent South, a jarring chord and a vague and uncomprehended cadenza has been and still is the Negro. And of that muffled chord, the one mute and voiceless note has been the sadly expectant Black Woman, ...

The "other side" has not been represented by one who "lives there." And not many can more sensibly realize and more accurately tell the weight and the fret of the "long dull pain" than the open-eyed but hitherto voiceless Black Woman of America.

. . . as our Caucasian barristers are not to blame if they cannot *quite* put themselves in the dark man's place, neither should the dark man be wholly expected fully and adequately to reproduce the exact Voice of the Black Woman.

—Anna Julia Cooper, *A Voice From the South* (1892)

The birth of the Afro-American literary tradition occurred in 1773, when Phillis Wheatley published a book of poetry. Despite the fact that her book garnered for her a remarkable amount of attention, Wheatley's journey to the printer had been a most arduous one. Sometime in 1772, a young African girl walked demurely into a room in Boston to undergo an oral examination, the results of which would determine the direction of her life and work. Perhaps she was shocked upon entering the appointed room. For there, perhaps gathered in a semicircle, sat eighteen of Boston's most notable citizens. Among them were John Erving, a prominent Boston merchant; the Reverend Charles Chauncy, pastor of the Tenth Congregational Church; and John Hancock, who would later gain fame for his signature on the Declaration of Independence. At the center of this group was His Excellency, Thomas Hutchinson, governor of Massachusetts, with Andrew Oliver, his lieutenant governor, close by his side.

Why had this august group been assembled? Why had it seen fit to summon this young African girl, scarcely eighteen years old, before it? This group of "the most respectable Characters in *Boston*," as it would later define itself, had assembled to question closely the African adolescent on the slender sheaf of poems that she claimed to have "written by herself." We can only speculate on the nature of the questions posed to the fledgling poet. Perhaps they asked her to identify and explain—for all to hear—exactly who were the Greek and Latin gods and poets alluded to so frequently in her work. Perhaps they asked her to conjugate a verb in Latin or even to translate randomly selected passages from the Latin, which she and her master, John Wheatley, claimed that she "had made some Progress in." Or perhaps they asked her to recite from memory key passages from the texts of John Milton and Alexander Pope, the two poets by whom the African claimed to be most directly influenced. We do not know.

We do know, however, that the African poet's responses were more than sufficient to prompt the eighteen august gentlemen to compose, sign, and publish a two-paragraph "Attestation," an open letter "To the Publick" that prefaces Phillis Wheatley's book and that reads in part:

> We whose Names are under-written, do assure the World, that the Poems specified in the following Page, were (as we

verily believe) written by Phillis, a young Negro Girl, who was but a few Years since, brought an uncultivated Barbarian from *Africa,* and has ever since been, and now is, under the Disadvantage of serving as a Slave in a Family in this Town. She has been examined by some of the best Judges, and is thought qualified to write them.

So important was this document in securing a publisher for Wheatley's poems that it forms the signal element in the prefatory matter preceding her *Poems on Various Subjects, Religious and Moral,* published in London in 1773.

Without the published "Attestation," Wheatley's publisher claimed, few would believe that an African could possibly have written poetry all by herself. As the eighteen put the matter clearly in their letter, "Numbers would be ready to suspect they were not really the Writings of Phillis." Wheatley and her master, John Wheatley, had attempted to publish a similar volume in 1772 in Boston, but Boston publishers had been incredulous. One year later, "Attestation" in hand, Phillis Wheatley and her master's son, Nathaniel Wheatley, sailed for England, where they completed arrangements for the publication of a volume of her poems with the aid of the Countess of Huntington and the Earl of Dartmouth.

This curious anecdote, surely one of the oddest oral examinations on record, is only a tiny part of a larger, and even more curious, episode in the Enlightenment. Since the beginning of the sixteenth century, Europeans had wondered aloud whether or not the African "species of men," as they were most commonly called, *could* ever create formal literature, could ever master "the arts and sciences." If they could, the argument ran, then the African variety of humanity was fundamentally related to the European variety. If not, then it seemed clear that the African was destined by nature to be a slave. This was the burden shouldered by Phillis Wheatley when she successfully defended herself and the authorship of her book against counterclaims and doubts.

Indeed, with her successful defense, Wheatley launched two traditions at once—the black American literary tradition *and* the black woman's literary tradition. If it is extraordinary that not just one but both of these traditions were founded simultaneously by a black woman—certainly an event unique in the history of literature—it is also ironic that this important fact of common, coterminous literary origins seems to have escaped most scholars.

That the progenitor of the black literary tradition was a woman means, in the most strictly literal sense, that all subsequent black writers have evolved in a matrilinear line of descent, and that each, consciously or unconsciously, has extended and revised a canon whose foundation was the poetry of a black woman. Early black writers seem to have been keenly aware of Wheatley's founding role, even if most of her white reviewers were more concerned with the implications of her race than her gender. Jupiter Hammon, for example, whose 1760 broadside "An Evening Thought. Salvation by Christ, With Penitential Cries" was the first individual poem published by a black American, acknowledged Wheatley's influence by selecting her as the subject of his second broadside, "An Address to Miss Phillis Wheatly [*sic*], Ethiopian Poetess, in Boston," which was published at Hartford in 1778. And George Moses Horton, the second Afro-American to publish a book of poetry in English (1829), brought out in 1838 an edition of his *Poems By A Slave* bound together with Wheatley's work. Indeed, for fifty-six years, between 1773 and 1829, when Horton published *The Hope of Liberty*, Wheatley was the *only* black person to have published a book of imaginative literature in English. So central was this black woman's role in the shaping of the Afro-American literary tradition that, as one historian has maintained, the history of the reception of Phillis Wheatley's poetry *is* the history of Afro-American literary criticism. Well into the nineteenth century, Wheatley and the black literary tradition were the same entity.

But Wheatley is not the only black woman writer who stands as a pioneering figure in Afro-American literature. Just as Wheatley gave birth to the genre of black poetry, Ann Plato was the first Afro-American to publish a book of essays (1841) and Harriet E. Wilson was the first black person to publish a novel in the United States (1859).

Despite this pioneering role of black women in the tradition, however, many of their contributions before this century have been all but lost or unrecognized. As Hortense Spillers observed as recently as 1983,

> With the exception of a handful of autobiographical narratives from the nineteenth century, the black woman's realities are virtually suppressed until the period of the Harlem Renaissance and later. Essentially the black woman as artist, as intellectual spokesperson for her own cultural apprenticeship, has not existed before, for anyone. At the source of [their] own symbol-making task, [the community of black women writers] confronts, therefore, a tradition of work that is quite recent, its continuities, broken and sporadic.

Until now, it has been extraordinarily difficult to establish the formal connections between early black women's writing and that of the present, precisely because our knowledge of their work has been broken and sporadic. Phillis Wheatley, for example, while certainly the most reprinted and discussed poet in the tradition, is also one of the least understood. Ann Plato's seminal work, *Essays* (which includes biographies and poems), has not been reprinted since it was published a cen-

tury and a half ago. And Harriet Wilson's *Our Nig,* her
compelling novel of a black woman's expanding consciousness in a racist Northern antebellum environment, never received even *one* review or comment at a time when virtually
all works written by black people were heralded by abolition-
ists as salient arguments against the existence of human slav-
ery. Many of the books reprinted in this set experienced a
similar fate, the most dreadful fate for an author: that of
being ignored then relegated to the obscurity of the rare book
section of a university library. We can only wonder how
many other texts in the black woman's tradition have been
lost to this generation of readers or remain unclassified or
uncatalogued and, hence, unread.

This was not always so, however. Black women writers
dominated the final decade of the nineteenth century, perhaps
spurred to publish by an 1886 essay entitled "The Coming
American Novelist," which was published in *Lippincott's
Monthly Magazine* and written by "A Lady From Philadelphia." This pseudonymous essay argued that the "Great
American Novel" would be written by a black person. Her
argument is so curious that it deserves to be repeated:

> When we come to formulate our demands of the Coming
> American Novelist, we will agree that he must be native-
> born. His ancestors may come from where they will, but we
> must give him a birthplace and have the raising of him. Still,
> the longer his family has been here the better he will represent
> us. Suppose he should have no country but ours, no traditions
> but those he has learned here, no longings apart from us, no
> future except in our future—the orphan of the world, he
> finds with us his home. And with all this, suppose he refuses
> to be fused into that grand conglomerate we call the "Amer-
> ican type." With us, he is not of us. He is original, he has
> humor, he is tender, he is passive and fiery, he has been

taught what we call justice, and he has his own opinion about it. He has suffered everything a poet, a dramatist, a novelist need suffer before he comes to have his lips anointed. And with it all he is in one sense a spectator, a little out of the race. How would these conditions go towards forming an original development? In a word, suppose the coming novelist is of African origin? When one comes to consider the subject, there is no improbability in it. One thing is certain,—our great novel will not be written by the typical American.

An atypical American, indeed. Not only would the great American novel be written by an African-American, it would be written by an African-American *woman:*

> Yet farther: I have used the generic masculine pronoun because it is convenient; but Fate keeps revenge in store. It was a woman who, taking the wrongs of the African as her theme, wrote the novel that awakened the world to their reality, and why should not the coming novelist be a woman as well as an African? She—the woman of that race—has some claims on Fate which are not yet paid up.

It is these claims on fate that we seek to pay by publishing The Schomburg Library of Nineteenth-Century Black Women Writers.

This theme would be repeated by several black women authors, most notably by Anna Julia Cooper, a prototypical black feminist whose 1892 *A Voice From the South* can be considered to be one of the original texts of the black feminist movement. It was Cooper who first analyzed the fallacy of referring to "the Black man" when speaking of black people and who argued that just as white men cannot speak through the consciousness of black men, neither can black *men* "fully and adequately . . . reproduce the exact Voice of the Black Woman." Gender and race, she argues, cannot be conflated, except in the instance of a black woman's voice, and it is this voice which must be uttered and to which we must listen. As Cooper puts the matter so compellingly:

> It is not the intelligent woman vs. the ignorant woman; nor the white woman vs. the black, the brown, and the red,—it is not even the cause of woman vs. man. Nay, 'tis woman's strongest vindication for speaking that *the world needs to hear her voice.* It would be subversive of every human interest that the cry of one-half the human family be stifled. Woman in stepping from the pedestal of statue-like inactivity in the domestic shrine, and daring to think and move and speak,— to undertake to help shape, mold, and direct the thought of her age, is merely completing the circle of the world's vision. Hers is every interest that has lacked an interpreter and a defender. Her cause is linked with that of every agony that has been dumb—every wrong that needs a voice.
>
> It is no fault of man's that he has not been able to see truth from her standpoint. It does credit both to his head and heart that no greater mistakes have been committed or even wrongs perpetrated while she sat making tatting and snipping paper flowers. Man's own innate chivalry and the mutual interdependence of their interests have insured his treating her cause, in the main at least, as his own. And he is pardonably surprised and even a little chagrined, perhaps, to find his legislation not considered "perfectly lovely" in every respect. But in any case his work is only impoverished by her remaining dumb. The world has had to limp along with the wobbling gait and one-sided hesitancy of a man with one eye. Suddenly the bandage is removed from the other eye and the whole body is filled with light. It sees a circle where before it saw a segment. The darkened eye restored, every member rejoices with it.

The myopic sight of the darkened eye can only be restored when the full range of the black woman's voice, with its own special timbres and shadings, remains mute no longer.

Similarly, Victoria Earle Matthews, an author of short
stories and essays, and a cofounder in 1896 of the National
Association of Colored Women, wrote in her stunning essay,
"The Value of Race Literature" (1895), that "when the literature of our race is developed, it will of necessity be different in all essential points of greatness, true heroism and
real Christianity from what we may at the present time, for
convenience, call American literature." Matthews argued that
this great tradition of Afro-American literature would be the
textual outlet "for the unnaturally suppressed inner lives which
our people have been compelled to lead." Once these "unnaturally suppressed inner lives" of black people are un-
veiled, no "grander diffusion of mental light" will shine more
brightly, she concludes, than that of the articulate Afro-
American woman:

> And now comes the question, What part shall we women play
> in the Race Literature of the future? . . . within the compass
> of one small journal ["Woman's Era"] we have struck out a
> new line of departure—a journal, a record of Race interests
> gathered from all parts of the United States, carefully selected,
> moistened, winnowed and garnered by the ablest intellects of
> educated colored women, shrinking at no lofty theme, shirk-
> ing no serious duty, aiming at every possible excellence, and
> determined to do their part in the future uplifting of the
> race.
> If twenty women, by their concentrated efforts in one
> literary movement, can meet with such success as has engen-
> dered, planned out, and so successfully consummated this
> convention, what much more glorious results, what wider
> spread success, what grander diffusion of mental light will
> not come forth at the bidding of the enlarged hosts of women
> writers, already called into being by the stimulus of your
> efforts?
> And here let me speak one word for my journalistic sisters

who have already entered the broad arena of journalism. Before the "Woman's Era" had come into existence, no one except themselves can appreciate the bitter experience and sore disappointments under which they have at all times been compelled to pursue their chosen vocations.

If their brothers of the press have had their difficulties to contend with, I am here as a sister journalist to state, from the fullness of knowledge, that their task has been an easy one compared with that of the colored woman in journalism.

Woman's part in Race Literature, as in Race building, is the most important part and has been so in all ages. . . . All through the most remote epochs she has done her share in literature. . . .

One of the most important aspects of this set is the republication of the salient texts from 1890 to 1910, which literary historians could well call "The Black Woman's Era." In addition to Mary Helen Washington's definitive edition of Cooper's *A Voice From the South,* we have reprinted two novels by Amelia Johnson, Frances Harper's *Iola Leroy,* two novels by Emma Dunham Kelley, Alice Dunbar-Nelson's two impressive collections of short stories, and Pauline Hopkins's three serialized novels as well as her monumental novel, *Contending Forces*—all published between 1890 and 1910. Indeed, black women published more works of fiction in these two decades than black men had published in the previous half century. Nevertheless, this great achievement has been ignored.

Moreover, the writings of nineteenth-century Afro-American women in general have remained buried in obscurity, accessible only in research libraries or in overpriced and poorly edited reprints. Many of these books have never been reprinted at all; in some instances only one or two copies are extant. In these works of fiction, poetry, autobiography, biography, essays, and journalism resides the mind of the nineteenth-century Afro-American woman. Until these works are made readily available to teachers and their students, a significant segment of the black tradition will remain silent.

Oxford University Press, in collaboration with the Schomburg Center for Research in Black Culture, is publishing thirty volumes of these compelling works, each of which contains an introduction by an expert in the field. The set includes such rare texts as Johnson's *The Hazeley Family* and *Clarence and Corinne*, Plato's *Essays*, the most complete edition of Phillis Wheatley's poems and letters, Emma Dunham Kelley's pioneering novel *Megda*, several previously unpublished stories and a novel by Alice Dunbar-Nelson, and the first collected volumes of Pauline Hopkins's three serialized novels and Frances Harper's poetry. We also present four volumes of poetry by such women as Mary Eliza Tucker Lambert, Adah Menken, Josephine Heard, and Maggie Johnson. Numerous slave and spiritual narratives, a newly discovered novel—*Four Girls at Cottage City*—by Emma Dunham Kelley (-Hawkins), and the first American edition of *Wonderful Adventures of Mrs. Seacole in Many Lands* are also among the texts included.

In addition to resurrecting the works of black women authors, it is our hope that this set will facilitate the resurrection of the Afro-American woman's literary tradition itself by unearthing its nineteenth-century roots. In the works of Nella Larsen and Jessie Fauset, Zora Neale Hurston and Ann Petry, Lorraine Hansberry and Gwendolyn Brooks, Paule Marshall and Toni Cade Bambara, Audre Lorde and Rita Dove, Toni Morrison and Alice Walker, Gloria Naylor and Jamaica Kincaid, these roots have branched luxuriantly. The eighteenth- and nineteenth-century authors whose works are presented in this set founded and nurtured the black women's literary tradition, which must be revived, explicated, analyzed, and debated before we can understand more completely the formal shaping of this tradition within a tradition, a coded literary universe through which, regrettably, we are only just beginning to navigate our way. As Anna Cooper said nearly one hundred years ago, we have been blinded by the loss of sight in one eye and have therefore been unable to detect the full *shape* of the Afro-American literary tradition.

Literary works configure into a tradition not because of some mystical collective unconscious determined by the biology of race or gender, but because writers read other writers and *ground* their representations of experience in models of language provided largely by other writers to whom they feel akin. It is through this mode of literary revision, amply evident in the *texts* themselves—in formal echoes, recast metaphors, even in parody—that a "tradition" emerges and defines itself.

This is formal bonding, and it is only through formal bonding that we can know a literary tradition. The collective publication of these works by black women now, for the first time, makes it possible for scholars and critics, male and female, black and white, to *demonstrate* that black women writers read, and revised, other black women writers. To demonstrate this set of formal literary relations is to demonstrate that sexuality, race, and gender are both the condition and the basis of *tradition*—but tradition as found in discrete acts of language use.

A word is in order about the history of this set. For the past decade, I have taught a course, first at Yale and then at Cornell, entitled "Black Women and Their Fictions," a course that I inherited from Toni Morrison, who developed it in the mid-1970s for Yale's Program in Afro-American Studies. Although the course was inspired by the remarkable accomplishments of black women novelists since 1970, I gradually extended its beginning date to the late nineteenth century, studying Frances Harper's *Iola Leroy* and Anna Julia Cooper's *A Voice From the South*, both published in 1892. With the discovery of Harriet E. Wilson's seminal novel, *Our Nig* (1859), and Jean Yellin's authentication of Harriet Jacobs's brilliant slave narrative, *Incidents in the Life of a Slave Girl* (1861), a survey course spanning over a century and a quarter emerged.

But the discovery of *Our Nig*, as well as the interest in nineteenth-century black women's writing that this discovery generated, convinced me that even the most curious and diligent scholars knew very little of the extensive history of the creative writings of Afro-American women before 1900. Indeed, most scholars of Afro-American literature had never even read most of the books published by black women, simply because these books—of poetry, novels, short stories, essays, and autobiography—were mostly accessible only in rare book sections of university libraries. For reasons unclear to me even today, few of these marvelous renderings of the Afro-American woman's consciousness were reprinted in the late 1960s and early 1970s, when so many other texts of the Afro-American literary tradition were resurrected from the dark and silent graveyard of the out-of-print and were reissued in facsimile editions aimed at the hungry readership for canonical texts in the nascent field of black studies.

So, with the help of several superb research assistants—including David Curtis, Nicola Shilliam, Wendy Jones, Sam Otter, Janadas Devan, Suvir Kaul, Cynthia Bond, Elizabeth Alexander, and Adele Alexander—and with the expert advice of scholars such as William Robinson, William Andrews, Mary Helen Washington, Maryemma Graham, Jean Yellin, Houston A. Baker, Jr., Richard Yarborough, Hazel Carby, Joan R. Sherman, Frances Foster, and William French, dozens of bibliographies were used to compile a list of books written or narrated by black women mostly before 1910. Without the assistance provided through this shared experience of scholarship, the scholar's true legacy, this project could not have been conceived. As the list grew, I was struck by how very many of these titles that I, for example, had never even heard of, let alone read, such as Ann Plato's *Essays*, Louisa Picquet's slave narrative, or Amelia Johnson's two novels, *Clarence and Corinne* and *The Hazeley Family*. Through our research with the Black Periodical Fiction and Poetry Project (funded by NEH and the Ford Foundation), I also realized that several novels by black women, including three works of fiction by Pauline Hopkins, had been serialized in black periodicals, but had never been collected and published as books. Nor had the several books of poetry published by black women, such as the prolific Frances E. W. Harper, been collected and edited. When I discovered still another "lost" novel by an Afro-American woman (*Four Girls at Cottage City*, published in 1898 by Emma Dunham Kelley-Hawkins), I decided to attempt to edit a collection of reprints of these works and to publish them as a "library" of black women's writings, in part so that I could read them myself.

Convincing university and trade publishers to undertake this project proved to be a difficult task. Despite the commercial success of *Our Nig* and of the several reprint series of women's works (such as Virago, the Beacon Black Women Writers Series, and Rutgers' American Women Writers Series), several presses rejected the project as "too large," "too limited," or as "commercially unviable." Only two publishers recognized the viability and the import of the project and, of these, Oxford's commitment to publish the titles simultaneously as a set made the press's offer irresistible.

While attempting to locate original copies of these exceedingly rare books, I discovered that most of the texts were housed at the Schomburg Center for Research in Black Culture, a branch of The New York Public Library, under the direction of Howard Dodson. Dodson's infectious enthusiasm for the project and his generous collaboration, as well as that of his stellar staff (especially Diana Lachatanere, Sharon Howard, Ellis Haizip, Richard Newman, and Betty Gubert), led to a joint publishing initiative that produced this set as part of the Schomburg's major fund-raising campaign. Without Dodson's foresight and generosity of spirit, the set would not have materialized. Without William P. Sisler's masterful editorship at Oxford and his staff's careful attention to detail, the set would have remained just another grand idea that tends to languish in a scholar's file cabinet.

I would also like to thank Dr. Michael Winston and Dr. Thomas C. Battle, Vice-President of Academic Affairs and the Director of the Moorland-Spingarn Research Center (respectively) at Howard University, for their unending encouragement, support, and collaboration in this project, and Esme E. Bhan at Howard for her meticulous research and bibliographical skills. In addition, I would like to acknowledge the aid of the staff at the libraries of Duke University, Cornell University (especially Tom Weissinger and Donald Eddy), the Boston Public Library, the Western Reserve Historical Society, the Library of Congress, and Yale University. Linda Robbins, Marion Osmun, Sarah Flanagan, and Gerard Case, all members of the staff at Oxford, were extraordinarily effective at coordinating, editing, and producing the various segments of each text in the set. Candy Ruck, Nina de Tar, and Phillis Molock expertly typed reams of correspondence and manuscripts connected to the project.

I would also like to express my gratitude to my colleagues who edited and introduced the individual titles in the set. Without their attention to detail, their willingness to meet strict deadlines, and their sheer enthusiasm for this project, the set could not have been published. But finally and ultimately, I would hope that the publication of the set would help to generate even more scholarly interest in the black women authors whose work is presented here. Struggling against the seemingly insurmountable barriers of racism *and* sexism, while often raising families and fulfilling full-time professional obligations, these women managed nevertheless to record their thoughts and feelings and to *testify* to all who dare read them that the will to harness the power of collective endurance and survival is the will to write.

The Schomburg Library of Nineteenth-Century Black Women Writers is dedicated in memory of Pauline Augusta Coleman Gates, who died in the spring of 1987. It was she who inspired in me the love of learning and the love of literature. I have encountered in the books of this set no will more determined, no courage more noble, no mind more sublime, no self more celebratory of the achievements of all Afro-American women, and indeed of life itself, than her own.

A NOTE FROM
THE SCHOMBURG CENTER

Howard Dodson

The Schomburg Center for Research in Black Culture, The New York Public Library, is pleased to join with Dr. Henry Louis Gates and Oxford University Press in presenting The Schomburg Library of Nineteenth-Century Black Women Writers. This thirty-volume set includes the work of a generation of black women whose writing has only been available previously in rare book collections. The materials reprinted in twenty-four of the thirty volumes are drawn from the unique holdings of the Schomburg Center.

A research unit of The New York Public Library, the Schomburg Center has been in the forefront of those institutions dedicated to collecting, preserving, and providing access to the records of the black past. In the course of its two generations of acquisition and conservation activity, the Center has amassed collections totaling more than 5 million items. They include over 100,000 bound volumes, 85,000 reels and sets of microforms, 300 manuscript collections containing some 3.5 million items, 300,000 photographs and extensive holdings of prints, sound recordings, film and videotape, newspapers, artworks, artifacts, and other book and nonbook materials. Together they vividly document the history and cultural heritages of people of African descent worldwide.

Though established some sixty-two years ago, the Center's book collections date from the sixteenth century. Its oldest item, an Ethiopian Coptic Tunic, dates from the eighth or ninth century. Rare materials, however, are most available for the nineteenth-century African-American experience. It is from these holdings that the majority of the titles selected for inclusion in this set are drawn.

The nineteenth century was a formative period in African-American literary and cultural history. Prior to the Civil War, the majority of black Americans living in the United States were held in bondage. Law and practice forbade teaching them to read or write. Even after the war, many of the impediments to learning and literary productivity remained. Nevertheless, black men and women of the nineteenth century persevered in both areas. Moreover, more African-Americans than we yet realize turned their observations, feelings, social viewpoints, and creative impulses into published works. In time, this nineteenth-century printed record included poetry, short stories, histories, novels, autobiographies, social criticism, and theology, as well as economic and philosophical treatises. Unfortunately, much of this body of literature remained, until very recently, relatively inaccessible to twentieth-century scholars, teachers, creative artists, and others interested in black life. Prior to the late 1960s, most Americans (black as well as white) had never heard of these nineteenth-century authors, much less read their works.

The civil rights and black power movements created unprecedented interest in the thought, behavior, and achievements of black people. Publishers responded by revising traditional texts, introducing the American public to a new generation of African-American writers, publishing a variety of thematic anthologies, and reprinting a plethora of "classic texts" in African-American history, literature, and art. The reprints usually appeared as individual titles or in a series of bound volumes or microform formats.

The Schomburg Center, which has a long history of supporting publishing that deals with the history and culture of Africans in diaspora, became an active participant in many of the reprint revivals of the 1960s. Since hard copies of original printed works are the preferred formats for producing facsimile reproductions, publishers frequently turned to the Schomburg Center for copies of these original titles. In addition to providing such material, Schomburg Center staff members offered advice and consultation, wrote introductions, and occasionally entered into formal copublishing arrangements in some projects.

Most of the nineteenth-century titles reprinted during the 1960s, however, were by and about black men. A few black women were included in the longer series, but works by lesser known black women were generally overlooked. The Schomburg Library of Nineteenth-Century Black Women Writers is both a corrective to these previous omissions and an important contribution to Afro-American literary history in its own right. Through this collection of volumes, the thoughts, perspectives, and creative abilities of nineteenth-century African-American women, as captured in books and pamphlets published in large part before 1910, are again being made available to the general public. The Schomburg Center is pleased to be a part of this historic endeavor.

I would like to thank Professor Gates for initiating this project. Thanks are due both to him and Mr. William P. Sisler of Oxford University Press for giving the Schomburg Center an opportunity to play such a prominent role in the set. Thanks are also due to my colleagues at The New York Public Library and the Schomburg Center, especially Dr. Vartan Gregorian, Richard De Gennaro, Paul Fasana, Betsy

Pinover, Richard Newman, Diana Lachatanere, Glenderlyn Johnson, and Harold Anderson for their assistance and support. I can think of no better way of demonstrating than in this set the role the Schomburg Center plays in assuring that the black heritage will be available for future generations.

INTRODUCTION

Barbara Christian

Mrs. A. E. Johnson's *The Hazeley Family* (1894) is somewhat typical of the "angel of the home" romances published by American women during the latter half of the nineteenth century—except that the author is a black woman, and her portrayal of the Hazeley Family is racially indeterminate, which in this country is generally translated as white. Her portrayal of the benevolent effects of Flora Hazeley's domestic and moral attributes on the well-being of her family reveals no overt signs that the novel's author is black. At first glance, it might seem that Mrs. Johnson has neutralized her tale so as to demonstrate that black women could write a sentimental romance in nonracial terms much the same way that white women did.

But Mrs. Johnson was not alone among Afro-American prose writers of the 1890s in her portrayal of solely nonracial characters. For example, three of Paul Laurence Dunbar's novels published between 1898 and 1901 are about such characters. This choice of character indicates one important aspect of the political-literary context within which these writers were constructing their novels. Afro-American writers used various tactics to overcome racial stereotypes like the smiling plantation darky that white publishers of the era demanded of "colored" writers. Charles Chesnutt, the most important Afro-American prose writer of the period, blamed his retirement from writing on such false stereotyping.

Readers should keep in mind that respectable girls and women of that period were not expected to work outside the home, for they would be subject to attacks on their chastity. Perhaps, then, in order to render her moral story about the qualities that young black respectable women—rather than stereotypical mammies or wenches—needed to keep their families intact and flourishing, Mrs. Johnson may have found it necessary to characterize her family in nonracial terms. Nonetheless, her treatment of the male characters in this story—the father who works on the railroad, the older Major Joe who has a modest vegetable trade—makes it obvious that her families are working and lower middle class instead of upper class and as such are subject to the many economic catastrophes that result when one of the breadwinners dies or goes astray. Mrs. Johnson does not portray most of her characters as comfortably well-off, a tendency among nineteenth-century women writers of sentimental romances. Rather, with the notable exception of widows who apparently inherited money from their husbands, her novel portrays families perennially subject to economic trials, a state in which black as well as white working-class families existed, although for blacks it was compounded by the effects of racism.

In her study, *Woman's Fiction: A Guide to Novels by and about Women in America, 1820–1870,* Nina Baym analyzes the fiction of American white women published during the middle of the nineteenth century. Although published in the last decade of the century, Mrs. Johnson's chronicle of the Hazeley Family conforms in some ways to the formulae that Baym outlines. *The Hazeley Family* is certainly based on the belief that "a happy home is the acme of human bliss," and that woman is central to the achievement of that acme.

The sixteen-year-old daughter of a small-town railroad worker and a "careless" mother, Flora Hazeley is brought up by her mother's sister, Mrs. Bertha Graham. Mrs. Graham is a kindly well-off widow who decides to train her niece according "to her own idea of what constituted education of a girl" since without it, Flora's situation would be worse off than her brothers'. Mrs. Graham is aware that, unlike Flora's brothers who have a choice of work situations in the world, the young woman will be limited to her role within the home, and that without a proper education in that realm, she will suffer as her mother did. Clearly the concept of an extended family is at work, while at the center of the novel is the theme of education—not only the kind of education a girl should have but also the *necessity* of receiving one if she is to be functional and happy.

Readers might assume that Mrs. Johnson emphasizes a traditional feminine education, and to a certain extent she does. Under Mrs. Graham's care, Flora's time is filled by "school, caring for the flowers in the garden, and dreaming under the old peach tree," in addition to the more mundane tasks designated by Mrs. Sarah Martin, Flora's other aunt, "the details of housekeeping, cooking, sewing, washing." But Mrs. Johnson sees such duties as only half a girl's education. After the death of her Aunt Bertha, and after she is unknowingly cheated of her inheritance by Aunt Sarah, Flora is plunged back into her mother's careless house where the second and perhaps most significant half of her education is realized. It is at this point that the novel begins. Johnson then stresses not only Flora's domestic skill but, more important, the development of her moral fiber.

It is that moral fiber that enables Flora to help keep her family together, a constant concern in Afro-American literature and life. No doubt the American Baptist Publication Society, which published the novel, strongly advocated the message that young black women must develop certain moral qualities in the context of homemaking. An advertisement of this publisher cited *The Hazeley Family* as a "book that should be in every Sunday-School Library." The black church was not alone in advocating this point of view. In preceding generations, black women activists like the ex-slave, Ellen Craft, put much energy into strengthening black families by training black women in domestic skills and homemaking, since the majority of these women had been field slaves and had had no house of their own to maintain before Emancipation. In post-Civil War black society, domestic skills were not only critical to black families' well-being but were also marketable skills for black women. In this novel, the emphasis is decidedly not on black women as wage earners (although in a destitute period, Flora and her reconstituted mother do earn their keep by sewing) but on the other important aspect of the homemaker, the capacity to create a nurturing and beneficial space within which the family might flourish.

When Flora is sent back to her mother, she is discouraged by the "neglected and untidy" house where there is no semblance of family. Selfishly, she is not concerned with the people around her, who are *her* family, but is engrossed by the loss of the home in which she grew up. Only when she is encouraged by the example of another sixteen-year-old, Ruth Rudd, and by a minister's homily that "whatsoever thy hand findeth to do, do it with thy might," does Flora find that it is "an actual treat to be busy," her first lesson in the development of her character. Flora takes action. She makes the Hazeley home a place where her father and her younger brothers want to be and thus protects them from the waywardness of the street. Flora affects both the young and her elders. Her example encourages her mother to change her ways while the sixteen-year-old passes on her values of godliness, caring, and homemaking to young girls. By making others happy, Flora becomes happy herself. Mrs. Johnson then makes it clear that a woman's domestic skills and feminine taste are not enough—it is her moral values, her selflessness and devotion that must be at the center of her homemaking.

Mrs. Johnson underlines the theme of Flora's education by including within it the story of another young woman's growth. When her mother dies, Lottie Piper also experiences the loss of her home. She is packed off to her sick aunt, who is cruel and from whom she runs away. Young girls are expected to take care of their older relatives, regardless of how they are treated. With Flora's guidance, Lottie learns not to be a coward, not to run away from her duty. Through gentleness, the young Lottie helps her aunt to change from a miserable old lady to a more kindly one. In both Lottie's and Flora's stories, young girls are mistreated by older female relatives, an indication that family ties do not conquer all. Yet it is through this mistreatment that both girls grow into practical, unspoiled women. At one point in the novel, Flora muses that if it were not for her Aunt Sarah's greediness she would not have returned to her mother's home and been put in a situation where she would become so resourceful and independent. And Mrs. Johnson implies that it is Lottie's service to her aunt that makes her a suitable wife for Alec.

In his introduction to the reissue of Harriet Wilson's *Our Nig* (1859), Henry Louis Gates, Jr., comments that this novel differs from those of nineteenth-century white American women in that Wilson's women characters are not mother figures to Frado, the beleaguered black protagonist—in fact, they are often hostile to her. This hostility is ostensibly due to the fact that the older women in Wilson's narrative are

white and see little resemblance, though they are women,
between themselves and Frado. Yet in *The Hazeley Family*,
which, like *Our Nig*, is set in the North, the friction between
the younger and older women is not due to race. Both Flora
and Lottie confront older female relatives who are not nurturing figures. However, the reasons for their hostility seem
to be societally determined. In both situations the older women
are frustrated and fear for their own well-being. Flora's Aunt
Sarah is concerned with her own economic fate, while the
misery of Lottie's aunt stems from illness and loneliness.
What Mrs. Johnson implies about both these women is their
lack of security and their alienation in a society that has little
space for them. The author underscores this theme by having
Lottie's aunt, once she learns that the young girl will be
married, express her fear that she will be left alone, the fate
of many elderly women. Young girls, then, are subjected to
the effects of the societal restrictions imposed upon older
women.

While the older women in *The Hazeley Family* are not
always good guides for the younger women, they are at least
substantive characters. In contrast, the fathers are shadowy
figures. We know little of Flora's father except that he works
for the railroad and then dies. Lottie's father goes West when
her mother dies, leaving her to be taken care of by her aunt.
Major Joe is an important older father figure in the novel,
but even he is estranged from his daughter when she marries
a man of whom he does not approve.

Family unity is not easily maintained and must be carefully
nurtured. Mothers and fathers die and children are scattered
about. Fathers, brothers, and sons move away to find work.
Female relatives cannot always be relied on to nurture the
young. Older women languish, ill and alone. The need to

secure the family is presented as an urgent one in this novel. Society does not provide any institutions to aid in the solution of some of these problems; hence the importance of the individual's role, that is, of Flora's role in reuniting Major Joe with his granddaughter Ruth Rudd, as well as Joel Piper with his sister Lottie. By becoming a selfless and resourceful woman, Flora effects not only the unity of her own family, but also that of other families. Thus she is not merely a homemaker but a social housekeeper, a role of increasing importance in black Northern communities that was often neglected by society in general, and one that women activists, black and white, undertook in their respective club movements of the 1890s.

But Flora is not the only one in the novel whose moral development is traced. In a subplot, Mrs. Johnson demonstrates how young men are threatened, when they leave home to work in other towns, by social vices—drinking, gambling, petty crimes. It is significant that just as the author focuses on younger women who lack older female guides because their mothers die or their female relatives are not nurturing, she also pays attention to young men who lack father figures. The story of Flora's brother Harry outlines his departure from home to work in another town after the death of his father and traces his fall into the sins of the street and his return like a prodigal son to the bosom of his family. His story parallels that of Joel, Lottie's brother, who also has left home, fallen, and repented. It is Joel, rather than an older man or a young woman, who helps Harry return to the path of virtue, just as it was Ruth Rudd who inspired Flora to become a dutiful daughter. Peers, rather than parental figures or romantic relations, help each other achieve adult development.

Johnson's exploration of the dangers of alcohol was not unusual among women activists of the late nineteenth century. Many of the temperance movement's constituents were women, black and white, who saw drinking and other aspects of city life as corrupting young men and threatening family life. Religious teaching as well as a rendition of the unhappiness caused by such a life are arguments that Johnson uses against these evils, and she emphasizes how family feeling is a bulwark against irresponsibility and waste.

In telling the respective stories of Flora's brothers, it is noteworthy that Mrs. Johnson contrasts the city-dweller Harry with Alec, the brother who becomes a farmer. He does have a father figure, Major Joe, from whom he learns farming. As a result, he remains throughout a sturdy figure who does not submit to the debauchery of city life. His portrayal points to the major positive imagery throughout the novel—that of nature. Clearly Mrs. Johnson is imbued with the sense that being in touch with nature is essential to social well-being.

At every turn, the author weaves flowers, fruit, and vegetables into her narrative. The novel begins with such an image: the sweet potato that Lottie gives to Flora and the growth of which becomes for her a talisman. That potato vine is replaced by more luxurious growth—the geraniums in Ruth Rudd's yard, Major Joe's vegetable trade, Alec's farm—as the author indicates how Flora is flourishing. Flora's name, of course, also participates in this schema. A beautiful and strong flower, she inspires others to grow. In contrast, when Mrs. Johnson wants to emphasize that something is awry, nature is bereft or neglected. Thus the yard of Lottie's aunt is brown and ugly; when the young girl runs away, she weeps under the long bare arms of an old poplar tree. In the writings of women in the nineteenth and twentieth centuries, especially Afro-American women, nature cannot be separated from human society. These two constructs, though apparently different, are interrelated. One has only to think of the titles of major Afro-American women's novels, from Jessie Fauset's *The Chinaberry Tree* to Alice Walker's *The Color Purple*, to realize how pervasive this tendency is in the literature of black women.

Of course, nature imagery is used in various ways by different writers. In many women's novels, nature is related, among other things, to sexuality and is sometimes even a code through which writers, hampered by social constraints, might indicate the sensuality of their characters. But Mrs. Johnson's chronicle of the Hazeleys does not dwell on any aspect of sexuality either in a natural or distorted state. There are no scenes of attempted or covert seduction, as might be implied in scenes in *Our Nig*. Even the men do not have sweethearts, angelic or otherwise. Only at the end of the novel is sexuality hinted at, but only in the context of marriage, and even then, both Alec and Lottie characterize their marriage in practical terms. Nor is bountiful nature in this novel associated with children. None of Mrs. Johnson's young people become mothers or fathers during the course of the novel. Perhaps Mrs. Johnson felt the constraints of stereotypes associated with black women—that they were wanton and constantly bore children—even as she wrote a novel using racially indeterminant characters. Also, Victorian concepts about fecundity, as well as the fact that her novel was published by the American Baptist Publication Society, might consciously or unconsciously have restrained her from dealing with these two significant aspects of woman's development.

Instead, Mrs. Johnson emphasizes through her imagery the naturalness of family and home and woman's place in it— that God and nature intended this to be the seed from which society proceeds. Without the careful nurturing of the family, human beings lead unhappy, fruitless lives. Perhaps the most succinct declaration of this point of view is found in Flora's thoughts when she must leave her Sunday school class: "Surely, the seed she had sown in their hearts would spring up, blossom, and bear fruit for the Master's kingdom."

In a more or less secular vein, Alec's closeness to the earth, his choice of farming as his profession, results in the financial stability that enables him to buy a house and begin a family. From that seed will sprout the continuation of both the Hazeley and Piper families. In the final scene of the novel, which takes place on Christ's birthday the families have a reunion and Alec and Lottie are married. The various themes of the novel converge in this scene. Harry, the prodigal son, has become a minister; Flora and her mother prosper by helping him save souls; Ruth Rudd raises eggs, a symbol of birth, and gives joy to her half-sister Jem (whose name provides the only hint of blackness in the novel) and to her grandparents whose farm is prospering; Alec buys a house and not only marries the practical Lottie but is able to take care of her aunt. Over this joyous union and rebirth, Flora, who has helped to bring all these people together, presides in happiness and peace.

In calling this chapter "A Homely Wedding," Mrs. Johnson eschews the conspicuously sentimental, romantic imagery of orange blossoms and satin that are desired by the comic Jem and that many young girls might associate with marriage. Instead the author highlights the solidity, godliness, and love at the Hazeley family core. She leaves us with the message that such a family can transcend misfortune and guarantee the happiness of its members. Mrs. Johnson, a Northern black woman living during the hard times of Reconstruction when hope might have been in short supply, might have chosen to make her message as palatable and available as possible to both black and white readers by relating it in an apparently race-free novel.

Hazeley Family.   Page 23.

THE HAZELEY FAMILY

BY

Mrs. A. E. JOHNSON

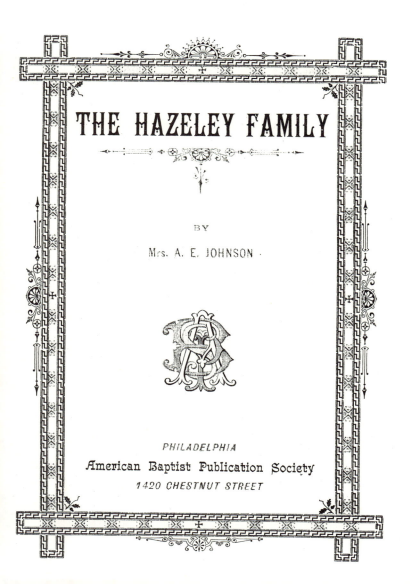

PHILADELPHIA

American Baptist Publication Society

1420 CHESTNUT STREET

THE HAZELEY FAMILY

BY

MRS. A. E. JOHNSON

Author of Clarence and Corinne

PHILADELPHIA

AMERICAN BAPTIST PUBLICATION SOCIETY

1420 CHESTNUT STREET

CONTENTS.

THE HAZELEY FAMILY.

CHAPTER I.

THE HAZELEY HOME.

SIXTEEN-YEAR-OLD Flora Hazeley stood by the table in the dingy little dining room, looking down earnestly and thoughtfully at a shapely, yellow sweet potato.

It was only a potato, but the sight of it brought to its owner, not only a crowd of pleasant memories, but a number of unpleasant anticipations. Hence, the earnest, thoughtful expression on her young face.

Flora was the only daughter. She had two brothers, one older and one younger than herself, Harry and Alec, aged respectively, eighteen and thirteen. The mother was of an easy-going, careless disposition, and seemed indifferent to the management of her household. Especially did she dislike responsibility of any kind. She was well pleased, therefore, to receive one day a letter from

her sister, Mrs. Graham, a childless widow, offering to
take Flora, who was then just five years old, promising
to rear her as if she had been her own daughter.

Mrs. Graham was well off. In her case this meant that
she lived in a pretty home of her own, with a nice in-
come, not only supporting herself in comfort, but per-
mitting her to provide a home for her elder sister for
many years, who had entire charge of the housekeeping. This sister, Mrs. Sarah Martin, was also a
widow and childless. The resemblance went no further,
for they differed, not only in manner, but opinions,
thoughts, and character.

Mrs. Graham, after a great deal of careful thought,
had come to the conclusion to adopt her little niece. In
fact she had often thought it over ever since the child
first began to walk, and call her by name. She was a
sensible woman, and it always annoyed her when she
would visit her sister to see the careless way in which
the children were being trained. Seeing this, she had
long wished to take and train Flora according to her
own idea of what constituted the education of a girl.

"It will be so much worse for her than for the boys,"
she had said one day to Mrs. Martin. "I do dislike to

see such a bright little child brought up to be good for nothing; and that is just the way in which it will be, if I do not take charge of her myself."

The latter clause was intended to draw indirectly from her sister an opinion of such a proceeding, for Mrs. Martin was by no means partial to children. However, it was received with the indifferent observation:

"Esther never did have any interest in children anyhow. She never had any idea how to take care of herself, much less anybody else," to which was added a remark to the effect that if her sister Bertha chose to burden herself with a troublesome child, she was sure she had nothing to do with the matter, and did not intend to have.

Mrs. Graham was rather surprised to have her suggestion received so coolly. She had expected a great deal of trouble in getting Sarah to consent, even provisionally. She was very glad to meet no more serious opposition, for, although she had fully decided in her own mind regarding the matter, yet her peace-loving nature dreaded unpleasant scenes. She purposely and entirely overlooked the expression of stern determination in the sharp-featured countenance of her sister, and

forthwith resolved to send for Flora without further loss
of time.

Thus it was that Flora Hazeley changed homes. She
was not legally adopted by her aunt, but was simply
taken with the understanding she would be returned
to her parents in case Mrs. Graham should in any
way change her mind, or weary of her charge. This
provision was inserted by Mrs. Martin, who determined,
in spite of her seeming indifference, not to be ignored by
her sister, upon whose bounty she considered she had a
primary claim.

For eleven years Flora lived in the pretty home of
her Aunt Bertha. Her time was filled by various occupations, school, caring for the flowers in the garden, and
dreaming under the old peach tree, which never bore
any peaches, but grew on contentedly in the farthest corner of the yard.

However, these were by no means the only ways in
which Flora spent her time, for Mrs. Martin, notwithstanding her stern resolve not to have anything to do with
her, had suddenly taken an equally stern determination to
do her share toward "bringing sister Esther's child up
properly."

This was fortunate for Flora. Aunt Sarah instructed her thoroughly and carefully in the details of housekeeping, cooking, serving, washing, in fact, everything she knew herself. How fortunate it was that she learned how to do these things, Flora realized some time afterward, as Mrs. Martin had intended she should. While she was learning them, Flora's progress was due rather more to the awe she felt of her stern aunt than to the desire to excel.

Mrs. Martin was ever ready to scold and find fault. Mrs. Graham never criticised, but always had a bright smile and something pleasant to say. As a natural consequence, she was dearly loved by her niece.

Mrs. Hazeley, Flora's mother, delighted to be relieved of her troublesome little girl, settled down more contentedly than ever, to enjoy the quiet of her daughter's absence, and became daily more and more indisposed to exert herself in order to make her home attractive.

It was usually pretty quiet now, because neither of the boys stayed in the house a moment longer than necessity demanded. Mr. Hazeley was employed on the railroad, and consequently was away from home a great deal. Mrs. Hazeley did little but turn aimlessly about, making herself believe that she was a very hard-working woman and then imagining herself much fatigued, found it necessary to rest often and long. She was at heart a good woman, when that organ could be reached, but possessed a weak, vacillating disposition, entirely lacking the gentle firmness of her sister, Mrs. Graham, or the uncompromising energy of Mrs. Martin.

Mr. Hazeley had long ceased to complain of his home and its management, for his words had no further effect than to bring upon himself a storm of tearful scolding, which drove him out of the house to seek more genial quarters. He was by nature a peaceable man, and when he found that neither ease nor peace could be had at home, remained there as little as possible. In fact, as Mrs. Hazeley's sisters had often said, "if the whole family did not go to ruin, it would not be Esther's fault."

Flora's life at her aunt's pleasant home had been a very happy one, and the time passed rapidly away. She was nearly through school, and looked eagerly forward into the future, that to her was so full of brightest hopes. It was her ambition to be of some use in the world. Just what she wanted to do, she did not know—

she had not yet determined; but that it was to be something great and good, she was confident, for small things did not enter into her conception of usefulness.

Aunt Bertha was her confidante for all her plans, or rather, dreams; she could do nothing without Aunt Bertha, for had not she the means? Flora felt sure nothing great could be done without money, that is, nothing she would care to do.

But, alas! Her summer sky, so promising and brilliant with hopes and indefinite plans, was suddenly overcast. Aunt Bertha was taken ill one day; the doctor said it was prostration, and he feared she might not rally. Flora was told. Her Aunt Bertha, whom she loved so dearly, and who loved her so much! Must she die? "I love her far more than my mother," she whispered to herself. This seemed very disloyal in Flora. But in truth, she had little cause to love the mother who had been so eager to relinquish her claim, and who, in all these years, had never expressed a wish to have her daughter at home.

During her sister's illness, Aunt Sarah spent her time in constant attendance upon her. She was cold, stern, and unapproachable as ever, giving the child little information in regard to the sick one who had been so kind to her. She was not allowed to enter the sick room during the first of her aunt's illness, although Mrs. Graham had often asked to see her niece.

One day, just before the spirit passed away, the sick woman called her sister, and said in a weak, trembling voice:

"Sister, I suppose you know I cannot live long, and that my will is made."

Mrs. Martin silently nodded.

"Well," continued Mrs. Graham, "I have left everything to you—I thought it would be best."

Again a silent nod.

"But, Sarah, I want you to promise one thing; that you will see Flora has what she needs to carry out her plans. The dear child has so longed to carry out some of her plans. I want her to have means to make whatever she may decide upon a success. And one more thing," she continued, pausing for breath, and looking pleadingly into the face above her, "I do hope, Sarah, that you will keep Flora here with you. Do not send her back to her home. I have left all I own in your hands, and I trust to you, sister, to do what I wish."

This long expression of her wishes had so taxed the fast-failing strength of the invalid, that she sank back, exhausted. No answer was expected, and Mrs. Martin was silent; and silent too, because she had not the slightest intention of doing as her sister wished. It was truly heartless; but Mrs. Martin was one of those people who do not present the harsh side of their nature in all its intensity until the reins of power are placed in their hands. So long as Mrs. Graham held the purse-strings, she acquiesced with as much grace as possible in her sister's plans. Was not the money Mrs. Graham's to do with as she pleased? It was quite a different thing, however, to feel that now everything would be in her hands to use as she chose. No matter if the donor was still looking into her face, her mind was made up that things should be ordered in the future according to her good pleasure. It was not at all her wish to burden herself with Esther's child, and forthwith she decided that back to her home Flora should go. However, she did not allow these unworthy thoughts to disturb the last moments of her tender-hearted sister, by giving expression to them. So good Mrs. Graham passed peacefully away.

Flora was allowed to see her shortly before she died. The kind voice whispered words of comfort, telling her that Aunt Sarah would take care of her. These words fell unnoticed at the time upon the ear of the sobbing girl, who had been so accustomed to have Aunt Bertha think and plan for her.

CHAPTER II.

FLORA AT HOME.

MRS. GRAHAM'S life had been a quiet, unobtrusive, but truly Christian one. She had neglected no opportunity to implant in her young niece a love and reverence for holy things; and now that she was about to die, she felt that she had nothing to regret, that she had left no duty unfulfilled, so far as Flora's training was concerned. It was with a heart full of peace that she commended her charge to the "One above all others" and took her leave of earth.

Flora was almost inconsolable. She had no one to comfort her, for Aunt Sarah was as distant as ever, being entirely too much occupied with plans for the future to care about Flora. Her mother came to the funeral, but neither was overjoyed to see the other after their long separation. It could scarcely be otherwise. Natural affection had never been conspicuous in the Hazeley home, and the influence of these years apart

15

had not helped matters at all. Indeed, they were little more to each other than strangers.

After they returned from the cemetery, however, Aunt Sarah informed Flora she was to return with her mother to her former, and as she deemed it, rightful home. The feelings with which the girl received this intelligence were by no means pleasant ones. But there was no use in crying or fretting about it, for when Aunt Sarah said a thing, she meant it, and could not be induced to alter her decision, even if Flora had felt inclined to ask her to do so. This she had no thought of doing, for she was not at all anxious to make her home with her cold, distant aunt.

"It is too bad!" she exclaimed, as she thought of all the bright helpful plans she and Aunt Bertha had made together, and which they had hoped to be able to carry out. "It is too bad!" she sobbed, as she bent over her trunk in her pretty little bedroom, the tears falling on the tasteful dresses, and the many loving tokens that had been given her by the dear hands now at rest beneath the unfeeling earth in the churchyard.

Mrs. Martin was surprised that Flora's mother made no objection to taking her daughter home. The truth was Mrs. Hazeley had been wanting this very thing for some time. It was not, however, because of any particularly affectionate or motherly feeling toward her child; but she had been thinking that Flora, of whose ability she had heard much, would be a very great help to her in caring for the house. Thus it was that Flora returned to the home she had left eleven years before.

Just as the train was preparing to leave the station, Lottie Piper, one of Flora's friends and admirers, came running to the car, and tossed something through the open window into Flora's lap, saying hurriedly and pantingly, as she pressed the hand held out to her:

"There, Flora, take that. Don't laugh. I raised it all myself, and I want you to have it; but don't eat it! Keep it to remember me by. Good-bye," she called, as the train moved off.

Flora waved her handkerchief out of the window to Lottie, until her arm was tired. As she looked about the cars her attention was attracted by a titter from the opposite side. At first she could not understand why the girl who sat there should look at her and smile. As her neighbor gazed at her lap, Flora's eyes followed, and

there she saw the cause of the merriment in Lottie's parting gift—a yellow sweet potato.

At first she felt inclined to be provoked with Lottie
for bringing such a thing and causing her to be laughed
at. However, the remembrance of her parting words,
"I raised it all myself; but don't eat it!" made her
smile in spite of herself. This encouraged the girl opposite to slip over to the seat beside Flora, as Mrs. Hazeley
was occupying the one in front, and the two girls,
although entire strangers to each other, chatted away
busily, until the train stopped at one of the stations,
where the girl and her father, who sat farther back, left
the car. Soon after, Flora found herself at home, Bartonville and Brinton being but a short distance apart.

This brings us to the opening of our story.

It was Lottie's potato that lay upon the table, and
Flora had been wondering what to do with it. The
memories it awakened were of Brinton and the many
pleasant strolls and romps she had enjoyed with Lottie in
her father's fields, which joined Mrs. Graham's, of
Aunt Bertha herself, and much more.

"But what am I to do with the potato?" she questioned. "I am not to eat it. I don't care to, either.

Oh! I know, I will plant it in a jar of water and let it grow. That would please Lottie, I guess."

She soon found a jar such as she wanted, and after washing it clean and bright, filled it full of clear water, and carefully placed the potato, end up, in it, and then looked about for a suitable place for it.

"That window has a good broad seat," she said to herself; "and it is sunny, but the glass is so grimy! However, it will do. Better yet, I will open the window."

This was more easily said than done, for, although the weather was still warm—it being September—the window did not appear to have been opened for some time.

Flora struggled and pushed, and at length succeeded in opening it, making noise enough as she did so, to attract the attention of a young girl who was passing. She stopped, looking up, inquiringly.

Flora was heated with her exertions and the thought of having attracted attention, so that before she realized what she was doing, she was smiling and saying:

"This old window was very hard to raise, but I was determined to do it."

"No," said the girl, looking as if she was not quite sure that it was the right thing to say.

"What is that in the jar?" she asked, as she came closer, and looked at the potato curiously, and then at Flora in a friendly way that pleased her.

"This," said Flora, patting the vegetable; "it is a potato."

"But what have you put it in there for?" persisted the girl.

"To grow, to be sure."

"Will it grow?"

"Of course it will," replied Flora, with an important air. "See! water is in this jar, and soon this potato will sprout, send roots down and leaves up, and then—and then—it will just keep on growing, you know." And Flora felt sure that she had put quite an artistic finish to her description of potato culture.

"Oh, yes," cried her new acquaintance, with an intelligent light in her eyes; "I know very well what will happen then."

"What?" asked Flora, rather dubiously.

"Why, little sweet potatoes will grow on the roots, of course."

"I—I don't think they will," said Flora, hesitatingly, not being well versed on the subject.

"Yes; but they must—they always do," returned the girl, positively.

"Well, but there would be no room in the jar for potatoes to grow," said Flora.

"That's so." And the girl looked puzzled; then they both laughed, not knowing what else to do.

"What is your name?" asked Flora, by way of changing the subject, for she was a little fearful she might be asked to explain why little sweet potatoes would not grow in her jar.

"My name is Ruth Rudd," was the answer. "What is yours?"

"Flora Hazeley."

"Is it? Well, I live just back of your house, on the next street. Good-bye. I guess I will see you some other time." And she hurried away.

"She is a real nice girl," Flora thought, as she turned away from the window; "I hope I can see her again."

She stood for an instant looking about the room. It was nicely furnished, but it looked neglected and untidy, and Flora, having been so long accustomed to the attractiveness and order of her aunt's house, felt home-sick. Her loneliness came over her in a great wave of feeling, and running through the kitchen, out of the door, went into the yard, which was a good-sized one, but so filled with rubbish and piles of boards, scarcely noticed through her tears, that she met with many a stumble before she reached the farther end. She wanted some quiet place in which to sit and think, as she used to do under the old peach tree at Brinton. She was sure she " could think of nothing in that house," and the best she could do was to seat herself on an old block at the very back of the yard. She felt she could think better out in the open air, under the sky, for she was a great lover of nature, and loved to look at the blue sky. The sun was under a cloud, but the air was warm and pleasant.

How different were her thoughts now from what they had been under the old peach tree! Then she had reveled in rose-colored dreams; now she was confronted by gray realities. Her thoughts went rapidly over her life since Aunt Bertha's death.

She had been here not quite a week, and she found it such a different place from the home she had so lately left, that she was almost unwilling to call it " home." But while she considered her present home not very desirable, she had given no thought to the inmates, whether or not they had found in *her* a very desirable addition to the circle.

She was young, and she soon wearied of her sombre thoughts, which could avail her nothing, and she glanced at the houses on each side of her own. There was a marked difference. It was not in the style of the building, for hers was the most attractive. It was, however, in the general appearance, and Flora felt she would like to begin at the topmost shingle and pull her home down to the ground. But the thought came to her that then she would have no home. She knew there was no room for her with Aunt Sarah, who was, no doubt, at this very moment enjoying her absence.

"No, indeed, I do not want to live with Aunt Sarah," she thought; and then began to wonder vaguely if she had not better go to work and try to make her present home a more congenial one.

The more she thought about it, the better the idea pleased her. Just as she was endeavoring to decide upon something definite to do, she was startled by seeing a board in the fence, just behind her, pushed aside. Before she could move, a round, fat, little face was thrust through the opening, and a pair of inquisitive brown eyes were fastened upon her. For a moment they looked, and then the owner squeezed through, and stood still, eyeing Flora complacently.

"Well, and who are you? and what do you mean by coming in here that way?" asked Flora, amused at the odd-looking little creature.

"I'm Jem," answered the midget, coolly; "and I didn't mean nuffing."

"Jem? I thought you were a girl," said Flora, looking at the quaint, short-waisted dress, that reached almost down to the copper toed shoes, and the funny, little, short white apron, tied just under the fat arms, which were squeezed into sleeves much too tight for them.

"So I am a girl," answered Jem, indignantly; "don't you see I've gut a napron on wif pockets in?" And she thrust her chubby little fingers into one of them.

"But you said your name was 'Jem,' and that's a boy's name," persisted Flora, enjoying her odd companion.

"'Tain't none," was the sententious reply; "it's short for 'Jemima'; that's what my really name is."

"Well, Jemima, what do you want in here?"

"Nuffing."

"Nothing? Well, that isn't in here."

"There ain't anythin' else's I can see," retorted Jem, turning down the corners of her mouth very far, and looking about disdainfully.

Flora laughed outright at this, but her visitor's countenance lost none of its solemnity.

"You do not seem to admire my yard, Jem."

"Don't see anythin' to remire," retorted Jem. "You'd just ought to peep in ours," and she moved over to the fence, and pulling away the board with a triumphant air, motioned Flora to look. Flora looked, but the first thing she saw was not the yard, but the young girl with whom she had been talking not an hour since.

CHAPTER III.

RUTH RUDD.

RUTH, standing by a long wooden bench, in the neat, brick-paved yard, was engaged in watering some plants that were her especial pride.

Hearing a noise at the fence, she turned, and recognizing Flora, smiled and asked:

" Won't you come in ? "

" Thank you," replied Flora, smiling in return. " I think I will."

Jem looked on wonderingly as her sister and the visitor, whom she considered her especial property, chatted.

She could not understand how they knew each other. At length, as they took no notice of her, she determined to assert herself; so, going up to Flora, she demanded:

" What do you think of *my* yard ? "

" Oh," said Flora, recollecting for what purpose they had come, " I like it very much indeed, Jem."

" It's a pretty good yard, I think," said Jem, with

much emphasis on the pronoun. "Come and look at the flowers, and I'll tell you the names of them." And she drew Flora nearer the bench.

"This is a gibonia," she continued, pointing with her fat finger to the flower named.

"You mean a 'begonia,' don't you, Jem?" said Flora.

"Yes," answered Jem, without changing countenance in the least, or seeming in any way abashed; "and this is a gerangum."

"A geranium," corrected Flora. "Yes, I see."

"And this is a chipoonia," pointing to a petunia, "and—Oh, there's Pokey!" and breaking away in the midst of her explanations, she gave chase to a fat little gray kitten that just then scampered across the yard, and into the house.

"What a cute little girl Jem is," said Flora to Ruth; "is she your sister?"

"Yes, that is, she is my half-sister; her mother was not my own mother, you know."

"Oh, she is your step-mother," said Flora.

"She was," corrected Ruth; "but she has been dead ever since Jem was a little baby. My own mother died when I was quite small," she added, with an elderly air.

"Who keeps house for you?" asked Flora, in surprise.

"I do," replied Ruth. "I keep house for father, and take care of Jem. She is all the company I have."

"What a smart girl you are. How old are you, Ruth?"

"I'm sixteen, but I feel ever so much older. You see, it is a great responsibility to have everything at home resting upon one," and Ruth looked very wise.

"I should think so," said Flora, thoughtfully. "I am sixteen too."

"Are you? That's nice. We ought to be good friends," returned Ruth, smiling.

"Yes, I am sure we shall be," replied Flora, earnestly. "I like you ever so much, Ruth. I am very lonely here. I know nobody in this place except my home folks."

"How strange," said Ruth, in a puzzled way. "Tell me about it."

Flora was glad to tell her story.

"You poor child!" exclaimed matronly Ruth, taking

her hand between both her own, and pressing it. " How sorry I am for you."

" Are you ? " said Flora, laughing nervously, for she felt more like crying. " I was just feeling sorry for you."

" Sorry for me ? Why ? "

" Because you have to live here all alone, or almost alone, and have so many responsibilities. You must get very lonely."

" Oh, but my responsibilities keep me so busy I have no time to be lonely. Besides, I like responsibilities."

" You do ? Perhaps if I had a few I wouldn't be so lonely either ; but then you see I have none."

" I think you have," returned Ruth, soberly, and added, after a moment's thought, " I think you have a great many."

" What are they ? "

" Your mother, and father, and brothers, and your home. You are responsible for your conduct toward your parents. It is your duty to be a good daughter. There's your home, it is your duty to make it pleasant and comfortable. And there are your brothers——"

" Oh, do stop, Ruth ! " cried Flora. " You have told me enough. You talk as if you were thirty years old instead of sixteen. No, no! I will not hear any more to-day about responsibilities; I have had enough for one day," and she playfully placed her hand over Ruth's lips.

"I wasn't going to say any more about them," said Ruth. "I was only going to ask you to come into the house, for I must begin to prepare our supper."

"No, thank you!" replied Flora; "I must go now; but I should like to come again soon."

"Indeed, come as often as you please; the oftener you come the better I shall like it. Come right through the fence whenever you want to; you will almost always find me here."

"Thank you," said Flora. She bade Ruth good-bye, and returned home the same way she had come, entirely unconscious of the look of disapproval with which little Jem was regarding her from the window of an upper room, whither she had retreated with her precious Pokey.

Jem felt quite slighted. Flora and Ruth had been so much occupied with each other as to forget entirely her important little self, and she determined to severely punish "Sister Ruth" for her conduct. She immediately proceeded to put her determination into execution by stowing herself and Pokey away in the darkest corner under the bed, and there she remained in spite of Ruth's coaxing calls.

Ruth found her there fast asleep, when she went to look for her at teatime. Ruth was well acquainted with Jem's various modes of punishing her, and she readily guessed the cause of her little sister's present displeasure; and likewise knowing her well, she decided to let her alone until she was ready to come down. At last Jem came down while Ruth was washing the dishes. She was in perfectly good spirits, for she felt satisfied that her sister had been sufficiently punished in having been deprived of her company for so long a time. She sat down quietly and ate her supper, which had been set aside for her. She did not say anything about the events of the afternoon and neither did Ruth, who was busy thinking about Flora. Strangely enough, influenced by some unseen power, Flora was at the same moment thinking of Ruth. When our young friend entered her home, she found her father had returned in her absence. Her mother was hurrying about in an aimless, impatient way, trying to get supper and at the same time set the table. These two occupations were not progressing very rapidly in her nervous hands.

Harry and Alec were both in the dining room; the former sitting by the window reading, and the latter whittling a bit of wood with his pocket-knife, and letting the chips fly and settle where they would. It was not a very inviting picture, but with Ruth's gentle face before her, and her words "It is your duty to be a good daughter" in her mind, Flora stoutly determined she would begin immediately and undertake her responsibilities in the very best way she could. With these thoughts she quietly said to her mother she would finish setting the table. It was not much to do, but she felt a great deal better in making this first effort to be of use in her home.

"What have I been thinking about not to have been doing this before? It is an actual treat to be busy," she continued to herself, as she placed the plates, cups, and saucers on the table. She did not know it, but both Harry and Alec were watching her whenever they were sure she was not looking.

The boys had not paid any attention to their sister since her return home; in fact, they both thought it a bother to have a girl about the place. Moreover, Flora had made no effort to prove herself a very valuable addition to the little family. But this evening, as she moved back and forth, the neat and tasteful way in which she arranged the table, was so different from the usual careless manner, that both boys were favorably impressed. Mrs. Hazeley too, when she hurried in with the supper, gave a sigh of relief, as she noted that everything was ready. And the father, although preoccupied with his own thoughts, glanced about with a pleased look in his eyes.

Although Flora was not aware of all this, she did not fail to notice there was a difference from the ordinary meal. The boys refrained from their usual snappish behavior, the mother was less peevish, and her father's face wore a look of quiet approval. On the whole, there was change enough to cause Flora to determine she would follow out the suggestion of her friend Ruth, and endeavor to make her home what she desired it to be.

When supper was over, Harry and Alec took their hats and went out, no one asking where they were going, or when they would return.

"How queer," thought Flora, who had volunteered to clear the table and wash the dishes, "how queer, that neither mother nor father seems to care where the boys

C

go, or what they do." And realizing the indifference of her parents, Flora began to feel an interest in the pursuits of her brothers.

When Flora retired to rest that night, she felt quite pleased with her experience of the afternoon and evening, and she intended that this should be the beginning of a new departure in her life ; and she felt glad that she had found such a friend as Ruth. She arose early the next morning, and was downstairs before her mother was stirring. It was Sunday, and the entire family were in the habit of rising later than usual on that day.

"What a dingy old place this is, to be sure," said Flora. "I'll make the fire and straighten things up a little."

When she had finished she looked about, and shook her head.

"It doesn't look a bit comfortable, or homelike. No wonder the boys go out every evening. I do wish I knew where to begin to improve things, but I don't, and I have no one to ask about it, except Ruth; yes, I will talk to her about things. Perhaps she can help me."

When Mrs. Hazeley came downstairs, to her surprise and unbounded delight she found the fire burning, the kettle boiling, and the table daintily laid, ready for breakfast.

"Why, Flora! I did not know you were up," she said, looking around, well-pleased with the generally improved condition of the room.

" I do believe your aunt has made quite a housekeeper of you," she continued, a moment later, as she inwardly congratulated herself upon the circumstance which had sent her daughter home.

Flora flushed at this unexpected, and for her mother, somewhat unusual word of commendation, but made no reply, for the simple reason that she did not know what to say. In spite of this feeling of pleasure that her effort was appreciated, she could not help wishing herself back in her aunt's home,—not as it now stood, with Aunt Sarah at its head, but as it had been under Aunt Bertha's gentle control. The more she thought of it, the more intense became the longing to be there in the old, happy, care-free life at Brinton. But there was nothing to be gained by wishing: Aunt Bertha was dead; Aunt Sarah was there, and there to stay; and she was at home, and here to stay; so there was nothing to do but to make the best of things, and get as much comfort out of

life as she could. Then she thought of Ruth's life, and
her brave effort to make a home for her father and Jem,
and inwardly Flora determined to emulate her example.
How well she succeeded the future will show.

CHAPTER IV.

FLORA'S FIRST SUNDAY.

BREAKFAST over, and the dishes cleared away, Flora looked about, wondering what else there was for her to do. Her father was reading a paper, and the boys had gone away. She went to the window where Lottie's potato stood in its jar. The sight of it carried her thoughts back so vividly to the old days, that she half resolved to look at it no more.

She felt dull and spiritless to-day ; it was no wonder, for there was little to make her feel otherwise. At Aunt Bertha's, every one had been accustomed to attend church, and Flora remained to Sunday-school. She had been converted and received into the church about a year before her aunt's death. Her sudden sorrow, her hasty trip from Brinton, and her unfamiliar surroundings in her new home, caused her to feel as if she had been removed to a heathen land.

None of the Hazeley household attended church, and Flora knew of no place to which she could go, for all was so new and strange to her, and being somewhat timid, she would not go alone.

Still standing at the window, and looking drearily out on the quiet street, she saw Ruth and little Jem passing, on their way to church. When they saw Flora they stopped, and she, glad to see a friendly face, hastened to open the door.

"Would you not like to come with us to church, this morning?" asked Ruth.

"Indeed I should," replied Flora. "I was just wondering what I was going to do with myself to day. Wait a minute; I will be ready in a very short time."

As good as her word, she was soon ready. "I am so glad that you stopped for me, Ruth," said she, as they walked along. "I know nothing about the churches here, and no one goes from our house."

"That is too bad," returned Ruth, sympathizingly.

Flora was indeed glad that she had come when, as they ascended the church steps, she heard the deep tones of the organ pealing out a welcome to all who entered. As they walked up the aisle, it seemed as if the sweet notes of the music twined around them, as though enfolding them in a loving embrace. A feeling of quiet content

filled the heart of the young girl, and for a time the realities were forgotten in the soothing sense of rest that stole
over her. Nor did she attempt to arouse herself until the
opening services were ended, and the minister arose to
announce his text.

In clear, distinct tones he read : " Whatsoever thy hand
findeth to do, do it with thy might." Twice he slowly
read the words, until Flora thought he surely must have
pressed them right into her brain, for she felt that they
were indelibly imprinted on her memory. Whether the
sermon was intended especially for young people, or not,
she did not know, but she felt that it was peculiarly ad-
apted to herself. I have no doubt that the older folks
felt the same with regard to themselves. It was one of
those texts and sermons that suit everybody.

" I wonder how many of my hearers can say truthfully
that they have done with their might ' whatsoever ' their
hands found to do," said the minister, looking, as Flora
thought, directly at her.

She dropped her eyes uneasily to the floor, and mentally
admitted, " I, for one, have not, unless it was to grumble
and fret with all my might. I have done that, but nothing else, at least since I came home."

"I am sure you cannot say that your hand has found nothing to do. You can perhaps say that your hand has not found what you wished it to do ; but that is not what the words of the text teach. It says ' *whatsoever* thy hand finds to do.' Then too, it is to be done ' with thy might ' ; not half-heartedly."

"Oh," commented Flora to herself, "why *should* he talk so straight at me? If he is not describing Flora Hazeley, I am mistaken."

"Did you ever notice," the minister continued, "that when you did a thing heartily, even though it was not the most agreeable occupation to you, it became more easy and pleasant to you?"

Flora thought of the little help she had voluntarily given her mother the previous evening, and again inwardly agreed with the speaker. The minister said a great many things that morning, some of which had never entered Flora's mind, and they made her very thoughtful; so thoughtful that she paid but little attention to the strains of the organ that accompanied her out of the church. She remembered he had spoken of many kinds of work the hands might find to do, and which were to be done faithfully and heartily. Perhaps it would be church work; perhaps professional work; perhaps mechanical work; and perhaps house-work and home-work. The last two, he thought, ought to go together, as neither could do very well without the other, although each differed in character. "House-work," he said, "as all knew, was sweeping, dusting, cooking, and the other duties connected with caring for the house; but home-work was the making and keeping a home; helping those in it to be contented and happy; brightening and making it cheery by both word and deed; shedding a healthful and inspiring influence, so that those around us may be the better for our presence."

"According to that, we *all* have a ' whatsoever,' " said Flora, emphatically to herself; "and the sooner I decide to start on my own part, the better it will be for me."

With her mind busy with many things, Flora was very quiet on her way home. The sermon to which they had listened was plain and practical. It was not brilliant, but it was helpful. The ideas were not necessarily new, but the words fell upon at least one heart already prepared and softened by circumstances to receive and profit by them. To Flora they were seed, falling upon the prepared ground of her heart, and in due time the fruit came forth. Most of the suggestions were new to her, for never before had she viewed them in this particular light.

Ruth respected her friend's silence, for she saw that she was busy with her thoughts, and guessing something of what they were, she was also quiet. Jem was unaffected by the silence of her elders. She walked along at Ruth's side, with her hand closely holding her sister's. Her happy life caused her every now and then to lapse from her dignified walk, and give a little jump and a skip. A continual volley of questions was thrown at Ruth, whose replies were not always as obvious as occasion demanded.

Jem's quick retort, "No, it isn't, Ruth," brought her to a realization of her abstractedness, and she resolved to be more attentive.

They left Flora at her door, Ruth asking if she had enjoyed the service, and added :

"Will you not come to Sunday-school with us this afternoon ?"

"I did enjoy the sermon very much," Flora replied, "and I shall be pleased to go to Sunday-school. If you will call for me, Ruth, I will be ready when you come."

A number of things grew out of Flora's experience on this Sunday. Its influence stayed with her, and had no small part in shaping her future life. She soon became an earnest worker to make the world better for her living in it; striving patiently and faithfully to render her daily life a power for good to those around her. How she succeeded our story will tell. Last, but not least, a strong affection sprang up between Ruth and herself, which proved a blessing to both.

Ruth taught a class in the Sunday-school, and persuaded Flora to consent to take one also, if the necessity arose. She introduced her to the superintendent, who welcomed her cordially to the little band of Christian toilers.

"One class is in need of a teacher," he said; "will you not take it? It is composed of girls from ten to twelve years of age."

"Oh, I should not dare to undertake a class of girls so old!" exclaimed Flora. "I am too young myself. Give me little girls, such as Ruth has."

"But," said Mr. Gardiner, "there is no such class in need of a teacher. Besides, it is not the age that has to do with your success as a teacher; it is the earnestness, perseverance, patience, and true piety which you bring to the work that will bring forth the results you desire."

"I am so inexperienced," murmured Flora.

"Neither has that anything to do with the matter," contended the gentleman, smiling. "Experience will come, all in good time," he added.

"Well," said Flora, "I will do my best."

"That is right," answered Mr. Gardiner, heartily. He felt sure that the young girl before him would succeed, for energy, conscientiousness, and determination could be read plainly in her bearing, and these, he knew, were characteristics of a successful teacher. He was glad, therefore, he had persuaded her.

Ruth, also, was pleased, for now her friend would be also a co-worker.

Flora felt sad when she thought that her family were the only ones of those who knew her who were entirely indifferent as to what she did or where she went.

"Only think, Ruth," she said to her friend, "it doesn't matter to them, whether I go wrong or right. What encouragement is there for a girl in my place to try to do right?"

"It does seem hard, dear," the gentle friend replied; "but then you will shine out all the brighter in the end for doing right in the face of discouragements; and God cares, you know."

They were at the gate, and bidding Ruth good-bye, Flora slowly went up the path to the house, her brain very active with new thoughts and purposes.

"Yes, God will help me, if I ask him," said Flora, softly, as she went to her room, and after doffing her hat and jacket, she knelt beside her bed, and asked the dear Lord to bless and strengthen her in her new surroundings, and let her life tell for him.

CHAPTER V.

THE BEGINNING.

MONDAY morning was cloudy. Flora felt gloomy and dispirited, and notwithstanding her good resolutions, not in a mood to make any extra exertion.

Mr. Hazeley had gone to his work, Harry and Alec to school, and the mother was in bed with a sick headache. Flora was lonely. There was much to be done, she realized, but just where to begin she did not know. There was no one to tell her what to do, and everything looked very dark to her on this Monday morning.

The dishes were nicely washed, and carefully put away. The little dining room had been swept and dusted, and looked somewhat more inviting. The window where the sweet potato, the last link binding her with the past at Brinton, stood, had been washed until the glass fairly shone, and now she stood gazing listlessly out into the street.

Presently she saw Ruth, on her way home from market. When in front of the house, Ruth looked up, and saw

Flora's woe-begone face at the window. She stopped, and gave her a smiling little nod. Flora's countenance brightened immediately, and she hastened to meet her.

"You look lonely, this morning," was Ruth's greeting.

"Indeed, I feel so," admitted Flora.

"If you are not busy come home with me for a while."

"I should like nothing better," cried Flora. "Just wait until I tell mother."

In a moment she was back, and the two walked on, Flora insisting on helping Ruth with her market-basket.

Jem met them at the door of the tiny house, and conducted them in with great dignity. Flora was delighted with everything.

"What a dear little house," she exclaimed, glancing about her admiringly.

"I am glad you like it," said Ruth, looking pleased.

"And what a dear, little, old-fashioned housekeeper you make!"

"Do you really think so?"

"Of course I do," said Flora, heartily. "Ruth, dear," she continued, abruptly changing the subject, "I want a talk with you."

"I shall be so glad to have you," said Ruth, seating

herself, with a pan of apples in her lap. "Sit down beside me, and you can talk while I pare these apples."

"I will help," replied Flora. "Run, Jem dear, and get another knife for me, like a good girl."

Jem obeyed, and soon returning, brought with her a box filled with bits of calicoes, and various odds and ends, seated herself also, and proceeded to fashion what she was pleased to call "doll's clothes."

"Ruth," began Flora, after they were all settled and busy, "I like you ever so much, and I hope we always will be friends. You seem to know so much, and you have had so much experience, that I am sure you can help me a great deal, if you will."

"Of course, dear," was her gentle reply, "I would be glad to help you all I can, and I shall be as pleased as possible for us to be friends. As to my knowing much, you are mistaken; I know but very little of anything; and experience,—well, I have had some, I suppose; but then, it isn't the sort that would help you, I am afraid. However, I shall be glad to do anything I can for you."

"I am sure you can help me, Ruth. You have helped me already," said Flora, decidedly. "And I mean to do as you suggested, and try to make my home just what I would like to have it. I don't know how to begin exactly; and then, mother never seems to care how things go, and that makes me feel as if I did not care either."

"I don't like to hear you talk about your mother so, Flora dear," said Ruth, in a troubled tone.

"How are you to help me, if I don't tell you just what I think and feel?"

"Perhaps, if you were to let your mother see and know that you wanted to help her, and make things bright, and talk with her——"

"Talk!" interrupted Flora; "I don't believe she would do it, even if I were to try."

"Oh, but *have* you tried yet?" asked Ruth, looking up archly. "You cannot tell until you do."

"Very well," said Flora, laughing, "I guess I shall try. But there is another thing," and the troubled look returned to her face. "It is about the boys, my brothers. They stay at home scarcely ever. I don't know where they go so often, and I am sure mother does not, and I don't believe she cares—you need not look grave again, Ruth—I don't. Harry and Alec seem to be good boys, and it is a pity they are not restrained. They may get into bad company—if they are not in it already—and do

D

something dreadful, and bring disgrace on us all. What can I do about that ? "

" It would take a wiser head than mine to tell you that," Ruth answered ; " but you might try and see if you could not make it so pleasant at home they would not care to be away so much."

" It seems pretty plain to me that that is easier to say than to do," retorted Flora, just a little impatiently.

" Yes, I know," assented Ruth, meekly ; " I don't pretend to be a Solomon ; I only said you might try."

" I don't believe they would stay for me," contended Flora, stubbornly.

" That is another thing you have never tried yet," said Ruth, smiling mischievously.

" That is so," laughed Flora, as she took two or three curly parings, and put them on Ruth's hair, to show penitence for her contrariety. " I guess I had better not talk any more, until I have tried to do something. I don't know how to begin my reformatory measures, but I suppose all will be well if I start with ' whatsoever.' "

By this time the apples were finished, and she rose to go.

" You haven't remired my doll's things," said Jem, reproachfully.

"So I have not," said Flora, and she sat down beside the little seamstress, and began to " remire " the various articles held up for inspection. She was compelled to see through Jem's eyes, however, for the shapes of the gar-ments were not so striking or familiar as to suggest their names.

When at length she reluctantly took her leave, Ruth invited her to come soon again, to which she laughingly replied she certainly should. After this, matters went on more pleasantly at Flora's home. She busied herself with making the house look as cosy and as attractive as the shabby furniture and worn carpet would admit. She suc-ceeded beyond her own expectations. She was gratified also that her brothers seemed to enjoy the improved con-dition of affairs, and so did her father when he was at home. Lottie's potato was now adding its mite to the general reform, and was sprouting nicely, sending its deli-cate white roots downward into the clear water, and its closely folded leaflets upward, to grow green in the warm sunlight. It seemed to be quite at home in the bright window. Flora had ceased to dream when she looked at her quaint friend. The days now, were too full to build air-castles. Mrs. Hazeley was pleased to shift her respon-

sibility to Flora, who enjoyed nothing better than to have
all her time occupied.   Often, when tangles would come,
Flora would run over to the ever-sympathetic Ruth, and
receive advice from her.   Thus, in being busy, Flora became more content, and often, as she thought of Aunt
Sarah, she knew she would not be found fretting.

She had not yet attempted to influence the boys by
word, but they soon noticed the new air of homeliness
pervading the rooms, and consequently did not go out so
much as had been their custom.   Alec, the younger boy,
was very mercurial and mischievous, while Harry, the
elder, was quiet, and fond of reading.

One evening Harry seemed to be more than usually
inclined to be sociable, and gave his mother and sister an
animated account of something that had happened " down
town," that day.   When he finished he took up his book,
and was just preparing to read, when Flora, eyeing the
volume distrustfully, asked :

" What are you reading, Harry ? "

Harry looked up at her quizzically, and answered her
question by another.

" Why ?   What is it to you, anyway ? "

" Nothing," said Flora, rather disconcerted.   She was

unaccustomed to boys, and had but little tact in dealing with them.

"I thought so," replied Harry, coolly, returning to his book.

"Will you not tell me what you are reading?" again asked Flora, not willing to be so easily vanquished.

"Why do you want to know?" demanded Harry, looking at her suspiciously.

Flora's lips again framed "nothing," but no sound came, for like a flash she thought, "If I say that, he will say, 'I thought so,' as he did before. No, I will give a reason," so she said:

"You seemed to be so interested in it, I thought it must be very entertaining."

"So it is," replied Harry, throwing a mischievous glance over to the corner at Alec, where he sat thoroughly engrossed in his favorite pastime of whittling, and in serene thoughtlessness allowing the clippings to fall according to their own sweet will.

Harry was confident that Flora intended to "read him a lecture upon trashy literature," as he afterward privately told Alec. He replied:

"It is interesting, Flo, about murders, and bears, cutthroats and burglars, and other horrors that would make you nervous to read about."

"I am not made nervous so easily as you may think, my dear boy," retorted Flora, condescendingly, and at the same time glancing cautiously at Harry, to see what effect this would have.

She had determined to try and gain an influence over her brothers, and felt that to show an interest in their occupations would be a good beginning. She realized the task she thus imposed on herself, but she meant to do her best, for this was another " whatsoever."

Harry was for a moment too much surprised to speak. Then he said, saucily :

"Ah, indeed ! Well, let me read some to you."

"I shall be glad for you to read to me, if you will read a story I have just started. I feel sure you will enjoy it. If yours is a book for boys only, I fear I could not appreciate it."

"Oh, you couldn't ? " said Harry. " Why not, may I ask ? "

But Flora was up and away ere the sentence was completed. Harry congratulated himself on having put her to flight, and returned to his book with a self-satisfied smile. Flora, however, had only gone to her room for a paper. Hurrying back, she spread it before astonished Harry, and, pointing to its columns, said, in a peculiarly persuasive manner :

" Now, Hal, I would be ever so glad if you would read that story aloud to us, while I crochet, and Alec whittles on the floor."

Alec looked confused, and began to pick up some of the litter he had made.

" Never mind, Alec," said Flora, laughing, " I will clear it up this time. Could you not put a newspaper under you to catch the cuttings, another time ?"

" All right," said Alec, looking relieved.

" We are all ready, Harry," said Flora, sitting down and taking up her work.

" Humph ! " said Harry, glancing carelessly down the page. " There's nothing in such a story. I don't want to read it. It is too flat."

" You are mistaken," replied Flora, spiritedly. " It's not a bit flat, and there is something in it. It is about a brave boy who saved a train."

" Oh, yes, I know," said Harry, skeptically, " and was not hurt."

"Yes, but he did get hurt. Why not read it, and see?" suggested Flora.

"Yes, read it, Hal," said Alec; "let's see what it is, anyway."

"All right," and Harry began to read with a comical nasal twang, very rasping to Flora's feelings, but she had the wisdom to say nothing. She was very glad, later, because Harry gradually dropped the false tone, and she could see by his manner that he had become interested, in spite of himself. Alec too, had ceased whittling, and was listening intently.

Forgetting to criticise, Harry read the entire story, which, in truth, was a pathetic little incident, very grace-fully and entertainingly told. He was silent, as he laid the paper on the table, but his thoughts were busy.

"I was right, was I not, Harry?" asked Flora.

"Yes," drawled Harry, smilingly, "you were. I did enjoy it, and I am glad you asked me to read it. But, let me see," he added, turning to the clock, "what time is it? Well," and he laughed, "I was good. It is nearly ten. Guess I will retire; I was going out, but it is too late."

Flora was secretly rejoiced to hear this, but she simply

said, "Good-night." She felt a glow of satisfaction as she realized a beginning had been made toward gaining the hold upon her brothers she so much desired.

"Flora, will you lend me that paper?" asked Alec, as she was preparing to go to her room. Flora willingly placed the paper in his hand, remarking, as she did so,

"I am glad you like the story. I have others, if you want them. Aunt Bertha kept me well supplied."

"Good night," returned Alec, and he was gone.

Flora was more nearly content than she had been for some time, as she sank into peaceful slumber that night.

CHAPTER VI.

"I BELIEVE I am going to realize some of the dreams I used to have, after all," Flora said to herself, as she laid her head upon her pillow that night.

She was right. The first step had been taken by her in the path of becoming an earnest worker, and to influence those about her as she had planned she would like to do, although not in such a way as this, nor in such surroundings. Her cherished dream of being instrumental in leading others into a higher and better life was now, she began to realize, leading her into the lines of duty in her own home, and among her own people. She could not wish for more.

She would not be like so many others, who in their desire to do great things, neglect the opportunities near at hand, and who, in longing to lead the heathen to a higher plane of life, forget those at home, who possibly for want of a word or act, have slipped, stumbled, and fallen on life's pathway.

Flora was growing, and with an earnest prayer to the Christ for guidance, strength, and tact, she cheerfully assumed more duties in the home, and greater responsibility. Her bright, sunny disposition, her pleasant face, her extreme willingness to respond to requests, gradually won a place for her in the hearts of those in her home.

The class in Sunday-school was assumed with a feeling of great apprehension. It was composed of five girls between the ages of ten and twelve. At first sight of their youthful teacher, these girls had been inclined to be displeased, but when they grew to know the sunny, sweet good-nature, born of the great desire to do them good, and which shone out of the earnest eyes, they loved her dearly. The teaching of this class was fraught with great good, both to the teacher and scholars, and this meeting with the eager, bright girls was soon eagerly looked forward to by Flora from week to week.

"How things have improved at Mr. Hazeley's!" soon grew to be a common remark among the neighbors.

"Yes, since Flora came home, it has become very different from what it formerly was," would be the spirit, if not the words of the reply.

Flora overheard a similar remark one day, and it gave

her a feeling of great joy to know the change was becoming apparent. Her resolution was strengthened to
sustain this newly made reputation.

It must not be supposed that she always had an easy
time. This was not so, for as she often said to Ruth,
"When mother and Harry are not in a good humor,
things do become tangled."

However, to do the family justice, they were beginning
to see and to more fully appreciate the changes made in
their home since Flora, who had left them a small
maiden, had returned with her thoughtful ways and mature manner. They forgot sometimes that she was but
sixteen, and would fancy she was older than she really
was. In fact, almost imperceptibly, she assumed all responsibility, and they deferred to her judgment in many
things. Best of all, however, they began to love her.

Her younger brother Alec seemed to have entirely
surrendered to her gentle, loving rule, and was ever willing to listen to her advice. He was always ready to
help her by running errands, chopping wood, drawing
water, and performing a dozen other little tasks quite
new to him, for he had never aided his mother in any
way. In fact she had never asked her boys to assist her,

or to save her extra steps or work, forgetting it ought to be required from them.

Mrs. Hazeley also had changed under the magic wand of Flora's sunny influence and determination to win the love of all. She had become at least a willing agent to the general change taking place in her home, and which recommended itself to her because her responsibilities were lightened and carried by other shoulders.

The house itself was transformed. Even cynical little Jem was becoming satisfied with it. It still contained the same furniture, but there was an air of comfort and home life about it never there before, but introduced by the magic of Flora's presence.

Lottie's sweet potato added its share to the general improvement which was going on. The long thread-like roots looked very white in the jar of water in which they were growing, and the graceful tendrils and light-green leaves were quite refreshing to the eyes. Flora had trained the vine about the window on small cords, and already it had nearly covered the lower part with its delicate branches. Flora would have felt lonely without it to care for; especially after being accustomed to have plants in profusion around her at her old home. Then

too, it carried her back to the happy days at Aunt
Bertha's, bringing a feeling of joy that she had been
permitted to live there so long, and to be trained in such
a gentle, firm, loving manner. Frequently she mentally
contrasted her care-free life there, and her life of responsibility now, and she determined, with the help that
is from above, she would not sink to her surroundings,
but would elevate them to her level. Bravely, patiently,
hopefully did she go forward with this end in view.

She was really surprised to find how fond she had
grown of her brothers, and they of her. She could
think of her mother very differently now, and she in turn
began to show signs of an awakening affection for her
daughter.

As to Ruth, she was ever the same, a quiet little home
body, whose hands were always too full to allow her to
come to Flora, but whose demure little face never
failed to smile a welcome to her friend, and whose wise
brain could turn over Flora's tangles and straighten
them.

The two girls loved each other dearly; and no safer,
truer friend and guide could Flora have found than
Ruth Rudd, who, although no older than she herself,

was very mature in thought, manner, and speech. Her face however, was childlike and innocent, reflecting the pure soul within. Flora was fortunate indeed in having her for a friend and confidante.

Harry Hazeley was a manly fellow with fine qualities. He had been allowed to do as he pleased, and had not been greatly benefited by this freedom. No restraining hand or guiding voice had been held out to him, or to cheer him on his way. Not being evil minded, he had taken but few wrong steps, and now his attention had been attracted to higher and better things.

As I have said, Harry had good qualities; one of which was a kind disposition, and although it was not always apparent to his every-day associates, was brought into play whenever he met any one who seemed in need of assistance.

One morning, as he was walking through the market on his way to school, his attention was attracted by an old man. One of his feet was swathed in bandages, and he was hobbling painfully back and forth, from his wagon to the stall, where he was trying to arrange a quantity of vegetables and some flowering plants which formed his stock in trade.

Harry had a quarter of an hour to spare, and he immediately offered to help the old man, who was only too glad to accept the proffered assistance, and who introduced himself, between the journeys from stall to wagon, as " Major Joe Benson, a gardener on a small scale."

Major Joe was an old ex-soldier, who had been wounded, and later imprisoned. The title " Major " was only a nominal one, and not indicative of any rank. His name, as he informed Harry, was Joseph Major Benson, Major being his mother's maiden name. He preferred to transpose this and call himself Major Joseph Benson, shortened for convenience to " Major Joe."

" It sounded sort of big, you know," he said, drawing himself up and looking dignified, until reminded by a sharp twinge in his foot that " rheumatiz " and dignity did not agree.

Major Joe was very talkative, and would not cease his persuasions until Harry had promised to drive out to his home with him some day, and see his nice little farm and Mrs. Benson, and he added :

" She will be delighted to see you, because you possess such a kind heart, and because you helped me. You must come."

"Yes, I will," returned Harry, "but I must be off to school now. Good-bye." And away he went, mentally pronouncing the major "a jolly old chap."

The visit was made, and strange though it seemed, a fast friendship sprang up between the two, and the visits became quite frequent. Harry had taken Alec with him several times, and he too had greatly enjoyed the trip. Major Joe could tell any number of quaint tales and reminiscences of interest to the brothers. Mrs. Benson, who was more active than her husband, was always desirous for Harry and Alec to remain to tea. Her heart had been reached by the kindness of Harry to her "Major," as she lovingly called him, and she could not do enough for them.

Harry had passed his old friend's stall a number of times since Flora's return, and had of course told him about his sister. The major had a strong desire to see this wonderful girl, as he deemed her to be, from the glowing descriptions that came to him. Finally he insisted, and Mrs. Benson sent in a kind invitation that the three, Harry, Flora, and Alec must come home with him to spend the afternoon and take tea.

He chose a beautiful day in early summer for the

visit, and Flora was anticipating it with no small degree
of pleasure, for it would be the first real holiday she had
had since coming home. The thought that the boys
cared enough about her to plan a trip for her was a very
pleasant one. Her mother seemed as much pleased with
the idea as the rest, and had insisted upon her going, so
Flora felt warranted in thoroughly enjoying her new experience. Mrs. Hazeley was daily becoming more energetic, and seemed really arousing to the fact that she had
a place to fill in her home.

Major Joe was to call for his three young friends on
his way home from market. He had promised to be on
hand by noon, and as punctuality was an economizer of
time, in the old gentleman's opinion, it was barely twelve
o'clock when he drew up with a great attempt at flourishing before the Hazeleys' door.

Hazeley Family.

Page 67.

CHAPTER VII.

A VISIT TO MAJOR JOE.

QUITE an effort was necessary in order to arrange the board for an extra seat for Flora and Alec. At length it was made ready, and Flora was helped in, and Alec followed, while Harry took his place beside the major, who commented as follows:

"So this is your sister, Harry? Well, well, she's a sister to be proud of; and I haven't a doubt but you are proud of her. Here, you Jacob, git up, will you?" and he shook the reins vigorously over his horse's back. "You never do come to a standstill but what you think it's meant for you to go to sleep."

Jacob, roused from his intended doze, lazily shook his fat sides, and slowly moved along. It was a lovely June day, and the little party had a very pleasant ride of about an hour and a half, Jacob not being inclined to hurry.

Major Joe was conversationally inclined, and nothing pleased him more than to hear the sound of his own voice. He chatted continually: now about the orchards they passed, and their probable yield of fruit ; now about the styles of the houses, as they came into view, and interspersed these remarks with reminiscences of the time when he was in the army.

The ride seemed quite a short one to Flora, who had enjoyed it thoroughly.

Mrs. Benson stood at the gate, watching for them ; and in her white kerchief and neat cap, looked good-natured and comfortable. A saucy little spaniel sat in the middle of the road, watching too ; and he was the first to catch sight of the wagon. He gave notice of the same by a sharp bark, and springing to his feet, doubled himself together, and bounded away, raising a cloud of dust in his haste to reach and greet his master. How happy he was when he reached the carriage! He sprang up at old Jacob, who paid no attention to such a small animal, but merely turned away his head with an air of supreme indifference.

" Jump, Dolby, jump ! " said Major Joe. After several ineffectual trials, and two or three hard falls into the dusty road, Dolby landed beside his owner, who had made room for him, and gave himself a vigorous shake, which sent the dust he had gathered in his long hair, over

Flora's clothes and into her face, causing her to choke, and a moment later to laugh. Dolby concluded this was in recognition of himself, and turning around, eyed Flora quizzically, and gave a satisfied little friendly bark.

The garden and nursery belonging to Major Joe were not large, but they were very fruitful, enabling him to realize considerable from the sale of his flowers and vegetables. He did not carry on his trade in a scientific manner, but merely for his love of the beautiful and useful things of the vegetable kingdom, and because to be inactive was for him to be unhappy. His receipts from the sale of the products of his land, together with his pension, enabled himself and Mrs. Benson to live very comfortably in their own snug little cottage, and, in addition, to lay aside something for a rainy day.

"Well, mother, here we are," said Major Joe, throwing the reins over Jacob's back.

"So I see," answered Mrs. Benson, nodding smilingly to the entire party. "Just come right in," she added, as Alec sprang out on one side of the wagon, and Harry helped Flora from the other.

The young people followed their hostess through the gate, and up the box-bordered walk into the cosy little

cottage.   Flora was soon seated in a low rocking-chair by
the window, whose broad sill was filled with potted
plants.

There Harry and Alec left her in good Mrs. Benson's
care, while they went for a walk over the place.

Flora soon discovered that her hostess was as sociable
as the major, and but a short time passed before they were
chatting like old friends.

By-and-by, Alec thrust his merry face in at the door,
and said :

"" Come out here, Flora ; the major wants you to see his
garden."

" Yes, dear, go, if you are perfectly rested," said Mrs.
Benson.   " I will stay here, and see about preparing our
early tea."

Flora joined her brother out of doors, and found Major
Joe and Harry waiting,

" Come and see my little green-house," said the old
man, waving his hand, and looking at them from over
his spectacles with an important air.   Flora complied
quite willingly, for she was very fond of flowers, and immediately won the major's good opinion with her enthusiasm over his pet plants, and the interest with which she

listened while he enlarged upon his management of them. The care of his garden was a tax upon his time, and really constituted quite a little labor. Then, outside, it was so pleasant to walk up and down among the neat flower-beds, in the small, but nicely kept orchard ; and in the kitchen garden, for the major prided himself on his choice vegetables, some of which frequently took prizes at the county fair.

The major himself was in his glory, for he had some one to whom he could talk. Talking was an occupation of which he never wearied, and now he chatted about the various departments of his labors, and how pleasant it was to watch the growth and development of the plants.

His tongue was still going very fast, when Mrs. Benson appeared in the doorway, and called to them that tea was ready. Reluctantly the old gardener relinquished his young listeners, who were, however, quite willing to vary the program, for they were hungry. The sight of the pleasant room, neat tea-table, and their genial, motherly hostess, was a very inviting one. In a lull of the conversation, during the progress of the meal, Mrs. Benson remarked, with a sad little smile, that Flora reminded her of her Ruth.

"So she does," exclaimed her husband. "I knew she made me think of somebody, but couldn't make it clear who it was."

"Is Ruth your daughter?" asked Flora.

"She is, or leastways she was," said Mrs. Benson, heaving a sigh, and adding, in a low voice, "She's dead now."

"I am very sorry," said Flora, with ready sympathy.

"Yes, our Ruth was a fine girl, but a little headstrong. We did all we could to make her happy and contented at home, but it seemed as if we did not succeed, and so, one day she ran off to marry a man we couldn't care for, because we were sure he wouldn't treat our girl kind— not that there was anything against him, but he was so cold and unfeeling. But she wouldn't listen to us, and went off, and we never saw her again."

"How sad!" said Flora; "but couldn't you go to see her?"

Mrs. Benson shook her head. "No; he said we were not to have anything to do with Ruthie, after he married her, and they moved away somewhere, we never knew where, until we heard in a roundabout way that she was dead." Here Mrs. Benson paused to wipe away a tear. "I had hoped she would at least have stayed near home, and been a comfort to us in our old age ; but, I suppose it's all right, and for the best. But excuse me for telling you so soon of our great sorrow. I should not have done it. Have you ever heard," she continued—and soon all were laughing heartily at her quaint sayings.

Flora, however, could not send from her thoughts this sad story. When the pleasant visit was drawing to an end, and they all were bidding Mrs. Benson good-bye, promising to come again, it still lingered with her. As old Jacob was soberly and deliberately trotting homeward, she revolved it over and over in her mind. Somehow it fastened itself upon her in a way she did not understand, and not until she was home, and had retired to her room for the night, did she arrive at even a partial solution of the perplexing problem. Then it dawned upon her with surprising clearness, that it certainly was because of the similarity of names in Mrs. Benson's daughter and her friend and adviser, Ruth Rudd.

This was very slight ground on which even to build an air-castle, but Flora did not stop to consider that, but in the midst of her dreaming resolved to go the next day, and rehearse to Ruth the story she had heard from Mrs. Benson.

Accordingly, next morning, after the work was done, and her mother was seated with her sewing, Flora donned her hat, and went to see her friend, expecting to find her busy as usual. She was, therefore, very much surprised to be met at the door, even before she had knocked, by Ruth herself, whose gentle face wore a troubled, anxious look, and she spoke in a low tone, as she responded to Flora's query :

" What is it, Ruthie ? "

" Father is very sick."

" Oh, I am so sorry ! What is the matter ? When was he taken ill ? Was it suddenly ? "

" Yes and no," said Ruth, answering simply the last question put by Flora. " He was compelled to stop work yesterday, and come home. He has been in poor health for a long time. I have been afraid, for quite a while, that he would break down."

" The doctor does not think he will die, does he ? " whispered Flora, in an awed tone.

" Yes, he does," said Ruth, as she wiped her eyes with the corner of her apron.

The two girls, with their arms entwined, and a deep tenderness in their voices, then went into the little kitchen, where Jem sat, holding her beloved kitten close to her for comfort.

"Yes, the doctor says that he cannot last long. But what bothers me is, there seems to be something on his mind, and I can see he is worried."

"What about? Do you know?" asked Flora, sympathizingly.

"Well, I can guess," Ruth answered, taking from a work-basket a stocking of Jem's, and beginning to darn it in an abstracted, mechanical way.

"You see," she continued, "father married my mother —my own mother, I mean—against her parents' wishes —she was young—and he never would be reconciled to them, because they had objected to him. Neither would he allow them to have anything to do with each other afterward. He was very stern, and it all made mother so unhappy it just broke her heart, I am sure. She died when I was very small. He has told me, since Jem's mamma died, he wished he had tried to pacify my grandparents. But he had moved far away from them, and now, if he should die, he has nobody with whom to leave Jem and me. But he was always so proud; and now we shall be all alone," and she gave a sorrowful little sigh.

"See here, Ruth," exclaimed Flora, a sudden thought flashing across her mind. "What was your mother's name?"

"Ruth, it was the same as mine," was the reply.

"Yes, but what was her last name?"

"Benson, I think."

"Well, then, I think I know your grandparents," cried Flora.

"You do? How? Where?" returned Ruth, in a puzzled, disjointed way.

"Wasn't, or isn't, your grandfather named Joseph Benson?" asked Flora.

"Yes, Joseph Major Benson; but how did you know?"

"Oh, I found out," was the answer. "And they live just a little way out in the country."

But, how do you know all that?" persisted Ruth, incredulously.

"Because I was there yesterday."

"Oh, Flora, are you sure? Don't raise my hopes and then disappoint me."

"My dear, you will not be disappointed; I should not like to do that," said Flora, gravely; "but let me tell you, and you can see for yourself." And then she told the story

Mrs. Benson had told her, ending with, "So, you see, there can be no mistake."

Ruth was delighted, and thanked her friend again and again.

"Just see how God works," she said. "Who can tell what he will bring about. How glad I am! I must not tell father anything about it just yet. We must manage to send word to grandfather, and have him here before we tell. It would not do to excite father unnecessarily; he is so very weak."

"That is so, Ruthie," said Flora; "you are wise, as usual, in thinking of that. I should have done quite differently. I should have rushed right in at once and told him."

"Not if you had been in my place," was the gentle answer. "You see, I have been accustomed to think about such things ever since Jem's mother died, as father never took much interest in the management of our household affairs."

After some more talk, it was arranged that Flora should go and bring Major Joe to see his son-in-law in the morning, and then the friends parted, Flora to hurry home and enlist her brothers' aid in her new project;

and Ruth to return to the bedside of her father, with the
pleasant hope of not only easing his mind, but the feeling that should he die, she would not be left entirely
alone in the world ; a possibility which she had dreaded
more because of her little sister, than on her own
account.

CHAPTER VIII.

MORE RESULTS.

WHEN Flora entered the house she found her
brothers there before her, and both very quiet. It
had grown to be such a pleasant thing to find their cheery
sister at home when they came in, that they had almost
unconsciously commenced to look forward to seeing her,
and hearing her merry voice. They hastened home
from school, and felt, but never expressed, disappointment
when she was not there.

Flora, while not yet so wise and thoughtful as her
friend Ruth, was daily learning lessons of usefulness, and
continually using and developing new powers heretofore
latent, and with her natural tact refrained from com-
menting upon many changes easily observed, going on in
the habits of her brothers. And now she simply smiled
at Harry, and pinched Alec's ear playfully, as she
passed him.

Then she went to her room to remove her hat, and
hastened back to help her mother with the dinner.

While putting the dishes on the table she imparted her news to Harry and Alec, between her trips from table to pantry. They were both well pleased to have the prospect of being able to brighten the lives of Major Joe and Mrs. Benson. They considered Flora very bright to come to the conclusion she did.

"I forgot all about that story soon after I heard it," said Alec, conscious stricken. "Didn't you, Hal?"

"I am afraid I did," laughed his brother. "But what else was there for me to do? I knew no way in which I might help, as Flora did."

"That's so," rejoined Alec, in a relieved tone, willing to share in his brother's self-absolution.

"Of course neither of you could have done anything, for you did not know Ruth. But tell me, what will be best to do?" asked Flora, pausing with a dish she was carrying to the table.

"I know," said Harry. "To-morrow is Saturday and market day also, and we all can go and see Major Joe in his stall, and tell him what we have heard, and what we think. If he is interested, one of us can stay at his stall while he goes and sees Ruth."

"How glad he will be; and how glad I am," said

Flora. " It would be dreadful for Ruth and poor little Jem to be left with no one to take care of them."

Thus the question was decided.

The next morning Major Joe was surprised by a visit from all three of his young friends, and none the less delighted to see them, however, because they came unexpectedly, and he gave them a hearty welcome. It was understood beforehand that Flora was to be the one to open the subject, and explain matters. She did not tell everything at once, as Alec thought she ought to do, but approached the object of their visit in a delicate way.

" Major Joe ; guess what brought us here to-day."

" I'm sure I can't say," answered the old man, rubbing his rough hands together, with a beaming smile. " Maybe to see your old friend ? "

" To be sure ; we're always glad to do that," replied Flora, as she placed the little bunches of parsley and thyme in more perfect order. " We have come for something else. Something very important," she added, seeing that Major Joe had no curiosity as to the nature of their errand with him.

" What would you say if I told you we had found somebody who belongs to you ? "

F

"To me?" queried the puzzled man. "I don't see how you could do that."

"Yes, but I have," said Flora. "I am sure of it."

The old major shook his head doubtingly.

"And I want you to come with me and see if what I said is not true," persisted Flora, coaxingly.

"But how can I?" questioned Major Joe in reply. "I cannot leave my stall—who would wait on my customers?"

"Why not let me take charge until you return," asked Harry, speaking for the first time.

"And I can help," added Alec.

"Now you see it's all fixed," said Flora.

"Surely you're not afraid to trust us, are you?" asked Harry, as he saw his old friend still undecided.

"No, no; it's not that, my boy; only——"

"Only nothing," interruped Flora, laughingly. "You must come, so say no more about it." And she caught his arm and led him away, an unwilling and unbelieving captive.

Ruth opened the door in answer to Flora's gentle tap. The latter could no longer restrain her impatience.

"Now, Major Joe," she exclaimed, softly, for fear of

disturbing the sick man, "whom does this little sober-sides remind you of?"

At first the old man looked from one to the other in a bewildered manner. Then his eyes rested on Ruth's face long and attentively. The tears gathered, and he involuntarily held out his hand, and said, softly, "Ruthie."

Scarcely realizing what she was doing, Ruth, probably drawn by the tender, loving tone that touched her heart, put her own in it.

"Who is she? What does it all mean?" asked the major, looking helplessly at Flora.

"It means," answered Flora, softly, "that this is truly Ruthie. Not your own Ruth, but her daughter and namesake—your grand-daughter Ruth."

"Is that so? Are you sure? Don't say so if you ain't," pleaded the old man. And then the thought flashed across Flora's mind that perhaps after all she was mistaken, and had only brought her old friend there to be disappointed.

"Ruth dear," she said, dropping into a chair, weakened by the very thought, "tell him—tell him all about yourself; your mother's name, and everything. Do, please, quick!"

Ruth told the history of her dead mother's life, as she had heard it from her own lips.

Eagerly Major Joe listened, and when she was through, he held out his arms to her, saying:

"You are my poor Ruth's daughter," and the tears prevented him from adding more. Ruth and Flora wiped their eyes in sympathy: Ruth rejoicing in the possession of a grandfather; Flora, that provision was thus made for Ruth.

This tearful trio was interrupted a moment later by the entrance of Jem, carrying her doll under one arm, and her beloved Pokey under the other.

"Why, Ruth Rudd, I'm extonished at you, hugging a old market man!" and Jem looked at her sister with unbounded disapproval.

"Hush Jem, you must not talk so," said Ruth. "This is our grandfather."

"Not mine," returned matter-of-fact Jem, standing still in the middle of the room, and looking suspiciously at the visitor. "Not mine. I never had any, and don't want one."

"Who is this?" asked Major Joe, looking at the defiant little figure dubiously.

"She is my half-sister," answered Ruth.

"Well, well," said her grandfather, "she ain't Ruth's child, so I've no call to take her when I take you, Ruth. Her father can send her to his own people."

"Then, grandfather, I cannot go with you," said Ruth, sadly, but firmly. "I will never leave Jem."

"Ruth, you're not going to leave me, are you?" cried the little girl.

"No, indeed, dear, I shall not leave you. It was not very nice for you to speak of grandpa as you did just now. You should always be polite to an old person. Remember this, Jem."

"I don't care," said Jem, defiantly. "He's horrid. He wants to take you away, and you're all I've got 'cept father, and—and he's going to die," she sobbed, hiding her face in Ruth's arms.

"Don't cry, Jem. I will not leave my little sister. What could I do without you?"

"No, no, little one, Ruth's grandfather won't part you, if you're so fond of each other." And the major came over and patted the sobbing child's head, soothingly. His was too tender a heart to withstand the sight of a child in distress, so it was soon settled that he was to be Jem's grandfather also, which arrangement was accepted by the little girl as readily as she had rejected the idea a moment before.

Then the major, his heart made very tender by memories of the past, was ready to visit the invalid.

John Rudd had always been a quiet man, but willful and determined to succeed in whatever he undertook. He was not bad at heart, and when a wrong act was committed it was invariably caused by obstinacy. He usually quickly repented of his course, and made all reparation in his power.

Knowing that Mr. and Mrs. Benson did not like him as well as he had hoped, he determined to marry Ruth, and to prohibit all intercourse with her family. In everything else he was thoroughly honorable, but he tenaciously held to this point. Ruth Benson, loving him devotedly, and believing all he said or did was infallible, implicitly obeyed this strange request without a question, and neither did she hear of or from her parents.

That the unnecessary sacrifice did not add to her happiness, was proven by the fact that she lost her free, light-hearted ways, and became quiet and melancholy, after a year or two of married life. Her husband was proud—too proud to admit that he had made a mistake, until it was too late for such an admission to do any good, and so after a few years she died, leaving behind her little namesake, Ruth. She seemed to have transmitted to the child in a large measure her own disposition, for Ruth was always a grave, silent, little thing, entirely unlike other children, and quite old for her years.

It was nice too, she possessed such a sweet disposition and even temper, for when her father brought home a new mother for the little Ruth, many changes were made in the home, and great would have been the discord but for Ruth's peaceful characteristics. Shortly after his second marriage, John Rudd moved to Bartonville, whether for business openings, or to be near the early home of Ruth's mother, no one ever knew.

Ruth knew the story of her mother's married life, of the home of her girlhood, and of the kind parents, but she did not know where the home was.

Whatever the reason for his coming, it was well for Ruth and Jem, for as I have said, provision was now made for them both at Major Joe's farm.

Ruth's life thus far, since the cares of the home were put upon her at the death of Jem's mother, had been an uneventful one. She had no companion but her little sister, who so filled her brain, and heart, and time, that she had no opportunity to grow lonesome. Personally, Ruth would have felt happier if her father had allowed the love, she doubted not he held for her, to find expression in a word of praise, a tender kiss, or appreciation of her efforts. But her father never thought of this longing of his daughter: he was so self-contained himself, and unemotionally inclined, that he could not have understood this craving, even had he known of its existence, which it is needless to say, he did not.

It was rather hard for so young a girl to persevere in her home-making with such a singleness of purpose as Ruth displayed, to give up her beloved studies without a sigh of regret, and to strive to train her younger sister, knowing she would receive no word of approbation from her father.

CHAPTER IX.

RUTH'S NEW HOME.

FLORA was very glad to know that at last her tender-hearted, patient Ruth had found some one to love her as well as to require of her duties. Love is a lightener of labor, and Flora felt that, in this respect at least, she was more fortunate than her friend. She felt sure, moreover, she was fast gaining the affection of her brothers and of her mother, who was gradually awaking to love for Flora and the desire to make the home attractive. She had something to work for. But Ruth—she had no one to whom to look for love, except Jem, as it was impossible to think of their quiet, undemonstrative father ever expressing any of his love for his daughters. One could only judge from his manner, for he never said much, and that was the same as when she first knew them.

John Rudd apparently took it as a matter of course that Major Benson came to see him as he lay ill, and expressed neither pleasure nor displeasure when he stated that should he not recover Ruth and Jem would be well cared for. He accepted, without feeling, the heartily expressed forgiveness from the major, thinking that perhaps it was due in some degree to the presence of two faces standing near by with earnest, pleading looks at the newly found grandfather, who, deprived of his daughter, would fill the vacancy in his heart with Ruth and Jem.

It was very difficult for Major Joe, with his tender heart, to leave his grandchildren. At last, however, he did, promising to return in the afternoon with Mrs. Benson, who would be overjoyed to see them, especially Ruth, who was so like her mother at her age.

As they returned to the market, Major Joe was prolific in his expressions of gratitude to Flora for her part in bringing about this delightful re-union, for had this not been done, Ruth and Jem would have suffered, and would have been left without parents or home.

Harry and Alec were well pleased with their new position, and because trade had been very flourishing during their period of power. Major Joe heartily thanked them all for their kind help to him this morning. Flora then returned home, but Harry and Alec remained to do anything else possible for Major Joe, as he wished to go home at once, and must pack his wares.

It is neither necessary to recount in detail all that pertained to the last hours of John Rudd, nor how attentive Grandfather Joe was to his newly found grandchildren; nor how overjoyed Mrs. Benson was when she first saw them. It will be enough to say that all that could be done toward rendering the dying man's last moments peaceful was done. Toward the last he roused, and in a simple, but earnest way, expressed himself content to die. He said that, although he had not spoken of the matter for fear of distressing the children, he had known for some time that it was to be so, and that long ago he had made his peace with God. He regretted his past careless life, both as to his duty to his Maker and to the children intrusted to him; "but," he continued, "God is good, and ever willing to forgive, and to accept a truly contrite spirit, and my trust is stayed on him." He expressed himself as very grateful to him for his goodness in providing for his children. He blessed them all with his last breath and passed peacefully away.

When the last sad rites had been performed, Ruth's

grandparents immediately began preparations to take her and Jem home.

The modest furniture of her home was entirely removed, although it somewhat crowded the cottage, but Ruth could not now part with these mementos of her former life, which had been her mother's.

At last, everything was ready, the little house was given up, and Ruth was spending a few moments with Flora, who, although instrumental in finding a new home for Ruth and Jem, was full of sorrow at the prospect of her loss in the parting with her friend.

"Don't look so sad, Flora dear," said Ruth. "Think what a blessing it is that poor little Jem and I have not been left altogether alone in the world. Had God not led you to find our dear grandparents, how very wretched we should be now. Besides, you know, we are not to be so far away; we can see each other often."

"That is true," returned Flora, brightening up; "I am glad of that; but it will be so lonely not to have you near me. Besides, I don't know any other girl as intimately as I do you."

"Oh, you will," said Ruth. "I am sure you will meet and become acquainted with some one as you did me.

I hope, if you do, you may be permitted to do them as much good as you have done me."

"And me too, Ruth," said an unexpected voice behind them.

Both turned, and saw Mrs. Hazeley standing in the doorway with a smile upon her lips and tears in her eyes.

"I used to be very unhappy, as you both know, and it was because I expected life to form itself for me—either for pleasure or unhappiness. Then Flora came," and she went over to her daughter and placed an arm about her, and looked lovingly in her eyes; "I watched her closely, and I soon discovered that she had determined to make this house a home, and a delightful one. No untoward circumstances seemed to discourage, but she was ever cheery and sprightly. We have gained by her home-coming—how much I cannot tell. She seems to have the mere power of will to mold circumstances as she chooses——"

"Not my will, mother," softly interrupted Flora, her face suffused with happy smiles; "it is God's will."

"Yes, yes, my dear," said Mrs. Hazeley, "I believe it. I want his will to mold my life too. A godless life is a wretched life, my children."

Harry and Alec had entered during the conversation, and were standing listening in amazement to what they heard from their mother.

"And the boys too," continued Mrs. Hazeley; "I am sure they have been helped by their sister's example."

"I know I have!" exclaimed Alec. Harry's only reply was to remark that the major was at the door waiting for Ruth. Then he turned and went out.

Flora felt a strange mixture of feelings at that moment. She was glad to know she had helped Ruth; unutterably grateful for her mother's words; and hurt at the seeming indifference of her brother. It was not her way, however, to dwell on what she could not prevent, so she only determined to strive harder than before to penetrate the armor of cold indifference worn by Harry of late.

As Harry left, they all went to the gate to wave a good-bye to Ruth. In the wagon was Jem, perched on a seat beside her grandfather, to whom she had clung with all the strength of her loving little heart. Immediately after the funeral she had gone home with him, taking "Pokey," and leaving Ruth in peace to pack.

This was really a comfort to Ruth, as Jem's presence would not have been of any great assistance.

Soon everything was settled, and with many injunctions to come soon, the party drove off, little Jem holding the reins with a steady hand, and a determination to drive all the way home.

A new life thus opened for the orphans, Ruth and Jem—a life of freedom from care, of joyous liberty to run at will in the garden of their grandfather, who delighted in the company of Jem, and who returned his affection in full measure. The life at the cottage was blessed by the loving guardianship of the grandmother, who saw in Ruth her own daughter of long ago.

Under this beneficent influence Ruth lost some of her seriousness, becoming more like other girls, and grew rosy and stout.

The life at the farm had so absorbed Jem's mind and time that, for the time being, "Pokey" was forgotten, much to the latter's satisfaction, for now she could lie in the sun and sleep in peace without fear of being unceremoniously awakened by her erratic little mistress.

Flora watched the wagon containing Ruth and Jem until it was out of sight, and then went into the house.

Alec and Harry had gone away. Mrs. Hazeley was sewing, and Flora, having no especial duty, and caring for none, went over and stood at the window, listlessly gazing into space. Her eyes soon dropped, and her attention was attracted by the yellow leaves on the sweet-potato vine. Flora felt as if all to which she had clung was leaving her in her loneliness. She looked closer. The potato was still firm and hard, and the jar was quite packed with roots, but the leaves on the vine were dying.

CHAPTER X.

LOTTIE PIPER.

FLORA had stood for some little time, mechanically caressing the vine, when she was surprised to hear near at hand, in a voice strangely familiar, the words:

"Well, I declare!"

Looking up quickly, but scarcely crediting her own eyes, she exclaimed:

"Lottie Piper!"

"Flora Hazeley!" returned the voice, and in a moment the friends were locked in each other's arms.

"Where did you come from? What are you doing here?" asked Flora, eagerly, in her desire to account for Lottie's presence in the village.

"Only one question at a time, if you please," laughingly returned Lottie. "Can you not guess?" she added, glancing at her gown, and for the first time Flora noticed it was black.

The quick tears sprang to Flora's eyes.

"Oh, Lottie, who is it? Not your mother?" she said,

sympathetically, her arm tightening in its grasp, and her thoughts running back to her sorrow when Aunt Bertha passed away.

"Yes," returned Lottie, sadly, " mother is dead. Father felt that he could not be happy at home, and so he went away out West, and left me with my aunt, Mrs. Emmeline Durand. And Flora, if you want to know what misery is, just you come and take my place for a while." And she looked at Flora with such a mingled expression of regret at her lot, and assumed resignation, that Flora was tempted to laugh, in spite of her sorrow in learning of the death of Mrs. Piper.

" If you want to laugh, you may," said Lottie, seeing her difficulty, and appreciating it, as was shown by the merry twinkle in her bright black eyes.

"No, no, I must not laugh," said Flora, squeezing her friend's arm affectionately. " I'm so sorry that your mother is dead. Where does your aunt live? I will come and see you."

" No, you—I mean you—can't—that is, she won't let you," stammered Lottie, blushing hotly.

" Yes, I understand. It is all right. It is not your fault," said Flora, hastily, appreciating the situation ; and wishing to relieve the embarrassment of the other, she added, "You can come and see me."

"I don't know," answered Lottie, glad to find that Flora understood. "I hardly think she would let me come. I have not asked her to go anywhere, as yet. I have been with her about five weeks, and this is the first time I have been out, except on an errand. She says she doesn't approve of girls 'gadding the streets.' I must go now. I have stayed longer than I ought to already, for I had a long walk before I saw you. Flora," she added, an instant later, as she glanced at the window, "isn't that a potato in that jar?"

"Yes," answered Flora, "it is the same one you gave me when I was leaving Brinton."

"Really? The very same?"

"Yes. You know you told me not to eat it, and I didn't know what to do with it at first. Then I thought it would look very nice if I put it in the window; I did, and it has grown splendidly and has kept green all winter."

"I am so glad you thought of that, Flora, because that was what I first noticed as I passed. And I thought it looked like a sweet-potato vine. And then, you know," Lottie continued, "if you hadn't I should not have stopped or seen

you ever, because I did not know where you were going when you came away. But what will my aunt say?
I guess I'll not get anything for supper but a bit of
tongue, and I don't fancy that, I can tell you. Good-bye."
And with a hurried kiss, and a warm embrace, Lottie hurried down the street.

She was sorry to go, as it was so good to meet somebody she knew—somebody connected with the old, happy
home-life, for while Lottie's mother lived, she had been
very happy. But now she was so lonely.

She hurried along the streets until she came to one
near the suburbs of the town. This street had trees on
either side, and was very quiet. The houses were small
and nearly all set back from the street.

Lottie walked along briskly, turning deftly in and out,
and at length arrived safe and sound at the little gate
leading into her aunt's yard. This gate opened upon a
small space, which doubtless had been intended by the
builder of the house to be beautified with flowers; but Mrs.
Durand's front yard was closely paved with red brick.
Not a flower, or a vine, or a bush broke the monotony,
which, however, was not wearisome, as the yard was small.

A high board fence enclosed the little yard on each side.

Close to the gate stood a large, old poplar, strangely drawn toward the quiet narrow street, as if weary of the unattractiveness of the house.

Lottie was nervous; she dreaded the reception she felt sure awaited her. The only thing that occurred to her to do was to knock, and she did so.

Receiving no response, she knocked again and waited. There was still no response, and thinking she had not been heard, she knocked again and again.

At length, just as she had decided that her aunt must be out, a calm voice from behind the door said in deliberate tones :

" If you will take the trouble to turn the knob, the door might open."

This idea had not occurred to Lottie, and the knowledge that the door was not locked somewhat confused her. However, she opened the door, and went in.

" There is a mat in front of the door," suggested the voice in the same slow, measured tones.

After wiping off the infinitesimal amount of dust from her shoes, Lottie timidly ventured into the room.

" Go to your room, if you will, and lay aside your wraps," came the voice, in an authoritative way.

Without speaking, Lottie obeyed. She felt as she slowly climbed the stairs that she had become a veritable automaton, without volition or energy, and compelled to do certain things. This grated on the sensitive nature of the girl, to whom, in the happy days that had passed, freedom to live in and enjoy the open air was everything. And now—and Lottie inwardly groaned at the thought —her actions were directed by one who seemed to forget her own girlhood, or that she had ever enjoyed the bright blue sky, the green fields, the merry; twittering birds, or the companionship of those who were of her own age.

Lottie had often wondered in her own mind if her aunt had ever been young, and if she had enjoyed her youth. There was no one to whom she could go for an answer. Had there been, Lottie would have been surprised to learn that she had been full of bright, merry fun, and had enjoyed life as she had at home.

"At home," Lottie thought, and paused, thinking of her mother, of the comforts and freedom of home, and then she looked in the glass to see if she was not old, for those happy days *did* seem so far away.

Mrs. Durand had met with many disappointments and a great deal of trouble in her life, of which Lottie knew nothing, and which had embittered her disposition, making her crabbed and disagreeable. As she now was, Lottie supposed she had ever been.

For some moments Lottie had looked in the glass, musingly. Now, as her thoughts returned to herself and her surroundings, she saw a dreary, woe-begone face looking at her from the quaint, cracked, old-fashioned mirror on her bureau. It was so doleful and forlorn, that Lottie nearly cried in sympathy with the miseries of the face before her. In a moment, realizing that it was her own reflection she saw, and enjoying her mistake, she laughed heartily, whereat the face in the mirror smiled pleasantly in return.

" Humph ! " said the voice downstairs.

" Oh dear ! " exclaimed Lottie softly ; " I have made her think that I don't care about staying out so long." And she slowly turned from the bureau and her mirth-provoking *vis à vis*, and leaving her room, slowly descended the stairs to her aunt.

The room in which her aunt sat was furnished very plainly. Some cane-bottomed chairs, a black horse-hair sofa, a small wooden stand, adorned with a red cloth on which was the family Bible ; two or three pictures upon the dingy walls, a pair of tall lamps with a bit of red flannel in the bottom, graced the mantelpiece. A dull ingrain carpet, and some home-made mats covered the floor. These, with a cloth-covered brick used to keep the door open, completed the furnishing of Mrs. Durand's parlor.

Mrs. Durand herself was a small, thin, wiry woman. Her features could hardly be called attractive; her lips were thin and tightly shut; her eyes were colorless, and she wore three stiff, little curls on each side of her face. She wore a dark gown, over which was a black apron, and on her head was a black lace cap. She was busily engaged in making another mat to adorn the floor, from long, bright-colored strips of cloth.

For some time she continued her work in silence. Lottie would have spoken had she had anything to say.

Presently, to Lottie's great surprise and relief, her aunt remarked:

"You may as well set the table, as you are here."

Lottie was glad to have something to do, as she was so much happier when employed.

"She hasn't scolded me yet, but it will come, that's certain," she said to herself, as she placed the dishes on the little round table in the back room which answered for both kitchen and dining room.

While at supper, Mrs. Durand questioned her niece about her walk, and Lottie told her, not forgetting the chance meeting with her friend, Flora Hazeley.

After supper, as was her duty, Lottie washed and put away the dishes, without further conversation with her aunt. That done, she took up a book and began to read.

CHAPTER XI.

CHANGES.

TIME passed on, and with it as usual came changes
The summer was gone and it was November, and
the weather was cold and dreary.

Lottie's life was much the same from day to day;
there was little variety to make the life of the young
girl pleasant. True, she did not have a hard time,
nor was she overworked, nor did she ever go hungry;
but the atmosphere of the house was always chill and
drear, and Mrs. Durand was as unsociable and unsym-
pathetic as ever.

It was perhaps true, that Lottie was somewhat prone
to slightly exaggerate her unhappiness, and to dwell
upon it until it seemed almost unendurable.

One morning, as she was dressing, she heard her
aunt call, and upon going to her room, discovered that
she was suffering from an attack of acute rheumatism.
Then, indeed, Lottie was sure her misery was at such a
height, that it could go no further.

As may be supposed, the sharp pain she endured did not render Mrs. Durand a more pleasant companion, and Lottie found that while it had been difficult to please her before it seemed utterly impossible to do so now.

Lottie did her best, with a determination pleasant to witness, and with the knowledge that it was her duty to care for her aunt under such painful conditions.

Lottie was lonely; she seemed to be entirely cut off from everybody she knew and cared for. She seldom heard from her father, and never from her brother, who had left his home when she was quite a little girl. She sometimes wondered if he was dead. She was industrious, and soon learned to keep house for her aunt very acceptably. She was not hard to please and was of a loving, sociable disposition. If her aunt had only made an effort to be agreeable and interested in her, Lottie would have been perfectly content.

If the months had brought but little change to Lottie, they had wrought a number of very important ones in the life of our friend Flora.

First, the news had reached them one day that the husband and father was killed in a railroad accident.

This, of itself, completely revolutionized affairs at the Hazeleys'. And then, just as they were trying to become a little accustomed to the sad change in the household, Harry disappointed them.

This was indeed a great blow, for Harry was, in a large measure, their main dependence. He was now about twenty years old and had been steadily at work for some time, and seemed on a good road to a successful business career. At first, he gave his earnings to his mother, only reserving enough to clothe himself neatly and comfortably, for he felt anxious to supply, as far as he could, her loss in the death of his father. This money, added to what Mrs. Hazeley and Flora made by doing plain sewing, and what Alec could earn out of school hours by keeping his eyes open, and his willingness to be of assistance to any one, was a great help toward keeping things going. For, although the little home was their own, of course there were the extra incidental expenses.

Mrs. Hazeley and Flora soon grew to depend on Harry, far more than they realized, until taught by his increasing fondness for remaining from home in the evening, and not unfrequently, all night. Great, indeed, was their sorrow when they learned how these evenings were spent—in the gambling house and the saloon. Had it not been for their hope in the Christ and his saving power, they would not have seen the faintest brightness in this cloud, which was a great burden to each, a sorrow about which they hardly dared speak.

Flora spoke earnestly and lovingly to her brother several times about the way he was conducting himself, but, as we have seen, he was not one to take this kindly, and knowing this, Flora felt she could do nothing but pray for her erring brother, who was so young, and yet so willful.

She never lost hope, nor did her firm belief that his better, nobler nature would prevail, weaken through those long, dark, hard days.

Mrs. Hazeley and Flora were compelled to devote all their attention to their work, as Harry could no longer be trusted to aid them financially; and, despite their brave, uncomplaining efforts, it was ofttimes difficult to make both ends meet.

Aunt Sarah had not visited them for some time, in fact, not since Flora came home, nor did they hear from her; and though knowing she might help them in their need, they could not bring themselves to inform her of their condition.

At length, one night they watched and waited for Harry to come home.

He did not come that night, nor the next, nor the one following; nor could they hear anything of him, except that he had not been around for days.

Where had he gone and what would he do? These were questions that Flora asked herself with a sick heart.

Mrs. Hazeley, with her naturally weak disposition, would have given way to despair under this new trouble and drifted back into the same condition in which we first found her, had it not been for her newly found trust and hope in her Heavenly Father, and the inspiring example of her courageous, self-reliant daughter. Flora seemed to grow stronger and more dignified under the added trials, and her mother, now a true Christian, was to her a great help and comfort; in fact, the two were all in all to each other, and the home that had at one time appeared to Flora most miserable, was now a haven of rest; and the mother from whom she had once turned away coldly, was now warmly loved and loving. Truly, there was sweetness mixed with her cup of bitterness.

Major Joe Benson, who had kept up his acquaintance with his young friends whom he greatly admired, and who by this time was considered quite a friend of the family, offered to take Alec to live with him. There was a very good school, he said, at no great distance from his home, and he would be glad to have the boy's help on his little place, especially now that Zeke was getting on in years, and had gotten above doing the many odd jobs he had performed when a boy, which state, while it was not many years distant, sufficed to make Zeke act, as Major Joe said, "very mannish."

No sooner was the proposition mentioned in Alec's hearing, than he was all enthusiasm, for nothing did he desire more than to live in the country. His mind was fully made up to become a farmer, and no recital of the hardships connected therewith, could divest such a life of its charms for him.

So it was settled, and it was really a great comfort to have at least one of the family well provided for, with the prospects of seeing him an upright and industrious man.

Now that provision was thus made for Alec, and he was but little expense to them, Flora and Mrs. Hazeley could manage very well by practising strict economy.

Life progressed very evenly and uneventfully, we might almost add happily, except for the sorrow caused by their ignorance of Harry's whereabouts.

One day, into their quiet and peaceful lives, very unexpectedly came Mrs. Sarah Martin, who was surprised at their comfortable surroundings.

She was greeted pleasantly by Flora and Mrs. Hazeley, who were determined to forgive and forget her treatment of them, but the warmth, which affection gives, was lacking. This did not fail to make itself manifest to Mrs. Martin, and, strange to say, instead of displeasing her, it seemed to have quite a softening effect upon her callous heart. The memory of this visit, and the picture of her niece's heroic efforts to keep her mother and herself from want, proved a veritable ever-present and sharp thorn in the side.

"Here I am, alone in the world, with plenty to supply all my wishes and some to spare," she thought one evening. We must do her justice; she was not miserly, but she was selfish—she wished to insure for her lifetime comfort for herself, and the gratification of her desires. "Here am I with plenty and to spare, while those of my own flesh and blood are struggling to keep the wolf from the door," she mused.

Having commenced to reproach herself she did not hesitate, for at every step seeing herself as others saw her, she discovered more cause to regret her attitude toward her sister.

"Have I been false to my trust?" she soliloquized, questioningly. "No—not exactly—because I gave no promise. And yet—Bertha supposed I would follow her request. However, I am not bound to do as she wished.

"Bertha would not have left me in charge had she supposed I would not carry out her wishes," she continued. "Probably she would not have given her property to Esther. She is so careless and extravagant that such a course would have been equal to her throwing the money away. Suppose the money had been left in trust to Flora? Would Esther have done more than I have done? No, she would have wasted it. What is the difference? Nothing; I am doing as Esther would have

H

done. Anyway, I will leave all to Flora, who will enjoy it after I am dead, and that will make it all right."

Another thing Mrs. Martin tried to argue in support of the idea that she had done all for the best, was that Flora had developed such astonishing qualities of self-government and ability. "She has almost made another woman of that mother of hers," she said to herself. "One can easily see that the material for a real, sound, sensible, practical woman is not in Esther, and if Flora were not there with her she would be the same as before, only worse."

There was a good deal of truth in what Mrs. Martin said. Some people cannot do or be anything without a definite motive, or an active example. But what did all this arguing amount to? Nothing at all, save to keep her mind in a constant state of turmoil, by her efforts to ease her conscience.

At last, with the constant strain she became mentally exhausted, and in spite of her efforts to the contrary for a long time lay upon the bed, a sufferer from nervous prostration. Her brain was unnaturally active, and she gained but little benefit from her enforced quiet. A neighboring physician was called, but found it impossible

to benefit her in her present condition. He might pre-
scribe medicines to meet certain symptoms in her case,
but he could not reach the seat of the trouble. She did
not consider that it was her business to add a description of her mental condition to that of her physical one.
She grew no better, and finally she decided to take a
course of .heroic treatment.

First, she proceeded to pay her physician and to inform him that she had no further need of his services,
much to that gentleman's disgust, who left muttering
that it was queer that the patient should be the one
to decide whether or not the doctor had been of service to her.

Next, she wrote in a feeble, trembling, and unintelli-
gible way, the following short, blunt note :

"NIECE FLORA :—I am sick. I want to see you.
"S. MARTIN."

Flora and her mother were sitting sewing very busily
that afternoon when the postman rapped on the door.

The sun was streaming in at the window, no longer
adorned by the sweet potato, which was long since dead,
but touching brightly the green leaves and scarlet blos-

soms of some geraniums—some of Ruth's "gerangums," according to Jem, that held the place of honor.

"From Aunt Sarah, mother," said Flora, carelessly, handing it to Mrs. Hazeley, who in turn read the short note.

"Well, Flora dear; what will you do about it?" she questioned, resuming her work.

"Oh, I guess I had better go and see her; hadn't I?" asked Flora, as she cut her thread.

"You may do as you please about the matter," returned Mrs. Hazeley, and there the matter dropped.

They continued their work in silence, their thoughts as busy as their fingers.

CHAPTER XII.

LED AWAY.

AND what had become of Harry Hazeley in all this time? Let us go back a little.

Probably all would have gone well with the lad, who was beginning to see a new life stretching out before him under the sunny influence of his sister, had his father lived.

While Mr. Hazeley exercised but little restraining power over his son during his life, the fact that he had a father had considerable influence over Harry. When Mr. Hazeley was killed, Harry realized that he was thrown on his own resources, and the fact that he was subject to no higher authority, took a firm hold upon him. At first, the idea aroused in him an innate, but undeveloped manliness, and he determined to stand by his mother and sister, and be a comfort to them as well as a support.

But the inherent weakness in his character soon gained the supremacy, and for the time over-ruled

117

all his resolutions, which had been made in his own strength.

It was inevitable that he should mingle with his companions in work, and soon they gained an influence over him that was not for his highest good. Being somewhat older than he himself was, they instilled into him a false idea of their superiority, and it was by this means they retained him in their "set"—a set of wild, dissipated young men.

Where was his judgment? Alas! he had inherited sufficient of his mother's weak disposition to over-rule it, and consequently, he was one of the kind most easily deceived and led.

One of the youths, whose name was Edward Hopkins, gained considerable influence over Harry. He it was who persuaded him to leave his mother and sister, and seek employment in another town, where, he said, work could easily be secured, with shorter hours and greater pay. This seemed very inviting to Harry, who, at that time, never thought of deserting his home, but was anxious to earn more money, and thus become better able to care for the family and have more for what he called pleasure—cards and gaming and wine, for he had now become addicted to the use of the latter, through whose insidious influence he was fast losing his manly bearing.

Poor boy! How many noble men has Satan conquered and then cast off? How many homes has he ruined, and hearts broken, and hopes destroyed?

But I am glad to say that I shall not be obliged to trace Harry Hazeley to the bottom of the pit into which he had fallen, for God had most graciously heard the prayers of his loving, trusting sister, who had first set the example of prayer to the mother, who now frequently joined her, and he was not permitted to reach its utmost depths.

True, he went down pretty far, and his rescue was effected by rather severe means; but what mattered that, so he was saved?

After leaving home, Harry plunged into his new, reckless life, with a strength that not only surprised, but very soon disgusted Hopkins, who wished to preserve the appearance, at least, of a gentleman.

Harry had been able to secure a first-class, remunerative position very readily, but so much went to satisfy his craving for excitement, that none was left to send

home to make life a little easier for Mrs. Hazeley
and Flora.

After a while, however, his increasing unsteadiness
secured for him dismissal from the shop where he had
been employed. He was fortunate in securing place
after place, but unfortunate in being unable to retain
them, until at length he did but little work and a good
deal of gambling. The work he then did was around
and about the saloons where he had chances to game and
drink.

One bitter cold night in December, a group of men
stopped in front of one of these places, and after some discussion, entered. It proved to be Harry's stopping place,
and he was sitting by the fire, for the time being idle.

To look at the sunken cheeks, restless eyes, and un-
cared-for appearance, one would never suppose this was
the once straight, tall, active Harry Hazeley, so greatly
was he changed.

The leader of the group of young men who entered the
bar-room appeared to be attracted by the forlorn figure
near the stove, as soon as he came in. He seemed to
know him, for presently he walked over to him and tap-
ping him familiarly on the shoulder, cried :

"Why, hello, old chap! How are you?"

Harry immediately recognized his old acquaintance, Edward Hopkins. He did not appear particularly glad to see him, however.

"Say, old fellow, you don't seem ready to shed tears of joy at seeing your old chum," remarked Ed, in a jovial tone, sitting down beside him.

Harry said nothing, but sat looking into the fire.

"Look here, now, Hal; you do look a little hard up. Haven't been getting along so well lately, I guess?"

"No, I haven't," said Harry, without turning around.

"Well, listen to me," resumed Ed. "The old proverb, 'a friend in need is a friend indeed,' is true, isn't it?"

"What of it?" questioned Harry, still apathetic.

"Just this," replied Ed, bringing his hand heavily down on his knee, "that I'm going to be a friend to you now."

Harry smiled incredulously. His confidence in the friendship of such a flashily-dressed fellow as Ed was, had been shaken.

"Come, don't be so glum, Hal. I've something to say to you," Ed continued, glancing around the room.

His comrades were all occupied in another part of the room.

"Now," went on Hopkins, lowering his voice, " we fellows," nodding toward the group, " are planning a little business. And if you want to, you can help us."

"What is it?" asked Harry, indifferently.

Edward took no notice of his manner, but went on :

"Well, we're going to—er—ah—walk into a small establishment, you know," and he winked slyly at Harry.

"Steal?" asked Harry, in a cold tone.

"If you like to put it that way, yes."

"Look here, Ed Hopkins," and Harry turned in scorn upon this hypocritical friend, who seemed so desirous of ruining him entirely. "Look here," he repeated, " let me tell you I don't want to share any of your 'little plans.' I've fallen low, I know, but I'm not a thief yet," and Harry straightened himself up and looked with a flashing eye into the crafty face beside him.

Hopkins was angry, as much because he had partially let Harry into his secret, as because he had refused to join him. However, he congratulated himself that he had not gone very far, and he left him abruptly, in a high temper, going over to the group at the other end of the room.

A heated discussion was progressing there about something in connection with the game of cards they were playing. They appealed to Hopkins as he joined the group. This did not seem to add peace to the scene, for the quarrel waxed hotter, and the voices grew louder.

Presently there was the sound of a scuffle, during which was heard the report of a pistol. Immediately there was a stampede, and when the officer, who had been attracted to the spot by the noise, rushed in, followed by a small crowd of men and boys, no one was to be seen but Harry Hazeley. He was lying on the floor by the stove, and gave no sign of life as the officer rolled him over. Whether the pistol had been fired accidentally or intentionally, nobody knew. The shot, however, was certainly not intended for the one who received it. It was found on examination that Harry was wounded in the side. He had also, in falling struck his head against the edge of the stove, and cut it.

"Well," said the officer, "I guess we'll have to take this young fellow to the hospital. From his looks he'll not be likely to have a better place to go to, even if he could tell where he belonged."

CHAPTER XIII.

WHEN Harry Hazeley returned to consciousness, he found himself in bed in one of the wards of a hospital, with his head bound up, and a dull aching in his side. He was in too much pain to wonder how he came there, so he closed his eyes and tried to go to sleep, but he could not. It seemed as if his mind had never been so active as it was now that he longed to forget everything, in the hope that this might ease his throbbing head. But that troublesome thing, memory, would assert itself, and his thoughts would travel back to the home he had left, and the sorrowing ones in it, and,—perhaps it was owing to the weak state of his system,—the tears forced themselves from underneath his eyelids, and rolled down his cheeks. But what is the good of thinking about these things? he mentally asked, and so he impatiently brushed the tears away.

Poor Harry had a hard time of it. He did not improve very rapidly, although he had the best of attention and nursing. His system was so poisoned by the use of alcohol, and he was so weak from having been so long without nourishing food that, while his wound was not a very serious one, it nearly cost him his life.

The pain from his wound, together with a low fever, racked his system until it was almost unbearable. His brain, however, was unusually active, and over and over again did he recall his life since he left home, and each time his repugnance grew; and when he began to convalesce, and he realized there was hope for him, he determined to lead a different life as soon as he was able to be around again. He sincerely and deeply repented of the past, and he felt the need of a Saviour, as he had never done before. He longed for some one to come and tell him of the Christ and of his saving power. He fully realized that he must have a helper, stronger than his will or his resolutions.

One morning, when Harry was getting a little more strength, there hobbled over to his bedside a crippled young man, who supported himself upon crutches. His body was distorted, and his legs were drawn up and twisted in a sad manner; but his face was bright and cheerful and intelligent, and his shoulders, arms, and hands had a look of manliness and strength about them that was greatly at variance with the feebleness of the rest of his frame.

" Well, friend," said this odd mixture of strength and weakness, as he seated himself slowly and cautiously by the bed. "Well, friend, how goes the world with you ? "

" I'm sure I don't know," replied Harry, drearily. " I haven't been caring much about the world lately. I ain't in much of a hurry to care either. There'll be time enough when I get out in it again."

" Time enough ! Time enough ! Yes, that's the cry," said the young man. " That's what has caused more mis- ery in the world than anything else; it's a rope that has lost many a soul forever."

Harry turned away impatiently. He did not want to hear.

" Of course you don't want to hear me talk that way," said the lame man bluntly, divining his thought. " I didn't suppose you did. But, let me tell you, young fellow, there's enough of that rotten rope left for you to lose your soul with. Will you turn your head away when you feel it snap, and find yourself dying, with nothing to hold on to,

I wonder?" Without more ado he grasped his crutches, and painfully hobbled away.

Harry tried to be glad he was gone. He did not succeed as easily, however, in dismissing from his mind the words he had heard. Perhaps it was the odd, abrupt way in which they were spoken, that made them fasten themselves so tenaciously on his memory. Certainly he would have been angry had any one else spoken so plainly and unceremoniously to him. The sight of his body, telling such an eloquent tale of suffering, made it almost impossible for any one to be angry with Joel Piper. Harry presently found himself wondering about him, and wishing he would come back and talk to him again.

He did not come, and one day Harry found courage to ask the nurse, who was busied near him, to tell him the name of the lame young man who talked to him one day.

"Oh, do you mean Joel Piper?" she asked in return.

"I didn't know that was his name," replied Harry, looking amused.

"Yes, it is," replied the nurse. "It's an odd name, I know, but he is just as nice as he can be. He's had a world of trouble and pain; but he's come out pure gold."

"Wasn't he always that?" asked Harry, curiously.

"No, indeed, he wasn't. He was one of the wildest young men, and it was that which brought on the sickness—rheumatic fever—which twisted him up so. It was this illness too, that brought about his conversion; and now he likes to visit the hospitals and talk to all the young men he can find, and try to get them to turn about. He says he's trying to make up for lost time. Some think he's crazy, but he isn't—only eccentric."

"Does he come here often?" asked Harry.

"Well, sometimes he does," was the answer. "Would you like to see him again?"

"I wouldn't mind having a little talk with him," admitted Harry.

"I'll tell him," said the kind woman.

Joel came; but Harry could not tell from his manner whether he was pleased or not at his having expressed a desire to see him.

Now that he was there, what should he say? Harry asked this question, but no answer came.

But Joel seemed to understand all about the matter, and began right away:

"You've had a rough time, eh? Didn't expect it, now, did you, when you started out? Going to have a good time, enjoy yourself, and all that? Well, it's all right. You've had about enough of that sort of thing, I guess. You'd like to turn right about face now, and go back to your mother, perhaps?"

"Who told you I had a mother?" asked Harry, sharply.

"Nobody," was the calm rejoinder.

"How did you know?"

"I didn't know; I only guessed. Somehow or other, you look as if you had. Have you?"

"Yes, I have," groaned Harry, "and a sister too; but I came away and left them, and now I'm ashamed to go back."

"Well, if you're made of the right kind of stuff you'll go to work as soon as you're out of this, and fix things so you'll not be ashamed to go back," said Joel. "Between us," he went on, bending over and looking at Harry with one eye shut up tightly, "I've got a mother and sister too. I did pretty much as you did, only worse, I guess. I've been working hard to make a man

I

of myself before I go back to them. I'm going soon too."

'To work!" exclaimed Harry, looking at the crooked figure pityingly. "What can *you* do?"

"Do?" repeated Joel, raising his brows, and opening wide his eyes. "Look," and he held up his long slim fingers. "I can write beautifully," he continued, with the simplicity of a child. "And I'm a clerk in a large clock and jewelry establishment. A good kind friend who came to see me at the hospital when I was so ill, secured the situation for me. And if you mean to turn about sure enough, and no going back about it, I will try and get you taken on as a salesman."

Harry was completely won by Joel's plain, straightforward manner and hearty kindness, and gave his promise to turn over a new leaf. What is of more importance he kept the promise faithfully.

When Harry was discharged from the hospital, he looked quite different from what he did when he first entered it, or rather when he was carried there. He was worn almost to a shadow, it is true; but his sickness had taken from him the look of the outcast, and his intercourse with his new friend, and the hopes he had for the future restored to him once more the ability to look the " whole world in the face."

He was clad in a suit that had been worn by Joel ere his body was so distorted by rheumatism. It was not a perfect fit, but it was clean and neat, and gave to Harry a very presentable air.

True to his promise, Joel tried and succeeded in getting the situation he spoke of for his young friend toward whom he had been strongly attracted.

Harry was also naturally smart and intelligent, and now that he had put off the shackles of the false friends with whom Satan had provided him, promised to do well in his new position. Joel was determined that through no fault of his should Harry fail. He never lost sight of him for any length of time. The two boarded at the same place, and Joel insisted on his accompanying him to church. They read, talked, and walked together, and as a natural consequence became much attached to each other.

CHAPTER XIV.

A CHAPTER OF WONDERS.

IT was a dull, gray, rainy morning when our friend Flora found herself standing in front of the house that had been her home for so many years.

What a flood of memories the sight of the familiar scene brought to her! She paused a moment or two to revel in the pleasure she thus felt. She did not feel at all excited, or even curious as to the cause for, or the probable result of her trip. Turning to the house, she stepped to the door, and lifted the knocker.

The door was opened by the neat, but uncommunicative maid, who was in charge of affairs during Mrs. Martin's illness; and who silently, and apparently acting on previous arrangement, let the way direct to the sick room.

Although the day was dark and cloudy, the window shades were down, and heavy curtains lent their aid to darken the room still more.

Mrs. Martin's greeting was somewhat of a surprise to

Flora as she stood on the threshold, scarcely knowing whether to enter the darkened chamber or not.

"Why don't you come in and shut the door?" came in fretful tones from the bed.

"I should like to do it, indeed, Aunt Sarah, if I could only see my way," returned Flora, mischievously. She wondered at her own temerity. At one time she would not have dared use such liberty of speech with this punctilious aunt. But she had grown to be very independent since she had been thrown so entirely upon her own resources, and had become accustomed to think and act both for herself and others. She felt that she had grown, in that she no longer stood in awe of Aunt Sarah's cold tones. Why should she? She had come to ask no favor.

"Well," came in questioning tones from the invalid.

"May I draw up the shades, Aunt Sarah?" asked Flora, advancing slowly into the room and closing the door softly.

"I suppose so. You can draw up anything you like, it makes no difference to me," was the somewhat ungracious reply.

Flora paid no attention to the tone, but drew up

the shades, making it possible to see what was in the
room.

"Aunt Sarah, how thin you are!" she cried, in-
cautiously. " Why, you have been sick."

" Of course I have. You didn't suppose I was pretending, did you ? ' retorted Mrs. Martin.

"No," said Flora, "I did not, nor did I know you
were so ill. And now tell me, can I do anything to render you more comfortable ? "

"No, I think not," she replied. "Yes, you might
bring me some toast and a cup of tea," she added a
moment later.

As she turned at once to leave the room, Flora wondered in her own mind, whether Mrs. Martin really
wished for something to eat. The truth was, Mrs. Martin, now that Flora was here in the house, even in her
very room, wished to decide how she could broach the
subject which had lain on her heart so long. She was
thinking deeply, and did not notice Flora's entrance
until she heard :

" Here they are, Aunt Sarah, nice and hot."

" What ? " the invalid returned, in a surprised way.

" The toast and tea," replied Flora.

"Oh yes, put them on the table."

Flora did so, daintily arranging them so as to be inviting to the eye as well as the palate, and inwardly wondering what new caprice her aunt would develop next. However, she had decided to yield to all her peculiarities, and to bear with her whims, and so with unruffled face, she turned to arrange the room, as only a woman's hand can. The grace and care were not lost upon her aunt, whose eyes closely followed every motion as she moved silently about the room.

"Sit down," said Mrs. Martin, after a few moments' silence.

Flora did so; and after a slight hesitation, Mrs. Martin began, having concluded to open the subject at once, for nothing was to be gained by delay.

"Niece Flora," she said, looking in the young girl's face, "I sent for you to tell you I feel that I have done what I had no business to do."

"What have you done, Aunt Sarah?" asked Flora, half suspecting what she wished to say to her.

"I mean in sending you away from here as I did," was the blunt reply.

"You had a right to do whatever you wanted to,"

stammered Flora. She could stand unmoved before the cold, hard Aunt Sarah; Aunt Sarah repentant, she did not know how to meet.

"No, I had no right to do it," continued Mrs. Martin. It was plain she did not intend to spare herself in the least. "I had no right to do it. Sister Bertha wanted you to stay, and I know she did. I had no right to take her money, and live in her home, and use her things when I knew she only left them to me because she trusted me to do what she wanted."

"Never mind, Aunt Sarah; I knew nothing about it, so do not worry. It is all right." And Flora moved nearer the bed, and took her hand in her own and tenderly held it.

Instead of complying, Mrs. Martin seemed to gain strength, and she went on:

"No; you knew nothing about her wishes, but I did. And, Flora, I have not been happy in this house. In fact, I did not deserve to be."

"You can talk about that when you get well."

"I will never be well unless I make right what I have made wrong," returned Mrs. Martin. "I want to know, Flora, if you can forgive your selfish old aunt for driving—yes, driving is the word," as Flora started to speak— "you from the home which was intended for you? Will you not come back to it?" And the tears began to gather in the eyes that had long been strangers to such an expression of emotion.

Flora felt very helpless now in the face of all these different moods. She could think of nothing else to do but stroke the sick woman's forehead gently and soothingly. After a moment or two of silence, she said: "I forgive you, Aunt Sarah, if you think there's anything to forgive. Everything has turned out for the best, at least so far as I am concerned. As to coming back, I think I don't care to—that is, I couldn't leave mother, you know."

"I don't want you to leave your mother, child. Why can't she come too?"

"Do you mean to come here to live?"

"Yes; here to live."

"She would like that, I know," said Flora, adding mentally, "providing you were different."

She soon discovered that her unspoken thought had been realized before it had been expressed.

"Now," said the sick woman, drawing a breath of

relief, "I can be at peace. It is not too late for me to make amends and carry out sister Bertha's wishes. Ah, child, you do not know what I have suffered of late; but it's all right now."

"Try to go to sleep now, won't you?" asked Flora, coaxingly, fearing the effect of the conversation upon the invalid.

"No; I don't want to go to sleep," said Mrs. Martin, with a shade of her old firmness; "I just want to lie here and think."

She did go to sleep, however, very soon, and awoke greatly refreshed, for her mind was at ease, and she was surprised to find how much more pleasant the prospect of recovery was since she had something to look forward to.

And Flora? She was delighted, for to her the old home had never lost its charm.

Faithfully she nursed the sick woman, who, in spite of her efforts to the contrary, now and then yielded to her old-time habit of fault-finding, when nothing pleased her. Mrs. Martin was very regretful for these outbursts, and after each, more carefully watched her own tongue, and the movements and manner of her young nurse and

daily became more attached to her; and the more necessary it seemed to her to retain her sunshiny presence.

Flora was as happy in her present position, and at her
future prospects, as it was possible for her to be with the
ever-present feeling of uncertainty and sorrow at the
absence of her dearly loved brother, from whom she had
expected such great things. She was a very sensible girl,
and had learned long before this that to waste her time
in worriment over what she could not help in any way,
would not enable her to discharge her present duties as
she would wish. Knowing this, as I say, so well, she put
Harry into the charge of the One "who never slumbers
nor sleeps," and went about her daily duties with a light
step and merry smile. For days she planned her mother's
coming, and how she would enjoy the life here. Her
own pleasant little room was hers again, and many were
the happy hours she passed there. Every few moments
throughout the day she would be in her aunt's room
reading to her, or perhaps giving her a daintily
arranged meal, or placing the pillows more comfortably.

One of her greatest pleasures was in arranging her
Aunt Bertha's old room, preparatory to the coming of

her mother, to whom she had assigned it. Very lovingly and carefully did she do this, for her heart was filled with tender memories of the past.

Mrs. Martin had told her to fix everything to suit herself, and refused to have a word to say further than to heartily approve of all her arrangements.

"I have been at the head of affairs a long time," she had said ; "it is time now for us to change places."

"I think you are trying to spoil me, Aunt Sarah," remarked Flora, one day, when she had been told a number of times to do just as she liked.

"I think there is no danger of that, my dear," said Mrs. Martin.

She was right, for the experience Flora had gained in the years since she had been home had so strengthened and developed her that it would have been well-nigh impossible to "spoil her," as she had termed it.

As soon as her aunt was able to sit up, Flora was to return home to get her mother, and in fact the whole family, if she could find them, and bring them to Aunt Sarah's, to live there.

Mrs. Martin insisted that she wanted a house full ; adding, smilingly :

" The more, the merrier, my dear."

Flora wished this could be possible—she longed to be able to bring Harry back with them; and, safe in that peaceful home, win him from his evil ways. She sighed, even as she thought, " That is quite impossible." She had forgotten for the moment that " With God, all things are possible."

CHAPTER XV.

DURING all these weary months, Harry Hazeley had not once written home; and neither his mother nor sister knew where he was.

His friend, Joel Piper, had written to his mother, but to his regret, had as yet received no reply. This saddened him, as in his letter he had told of the changes in him, not only in his body, but in his heart and life, for he wished his mother, who had done so much for him, to know.

Harry as yet had no news to write home. Joel was working slowly, it is true, to induce Harry to attend some meetings which were being held successively in different churches. Harry became interested, and later he had the happiness of knowing that he had accepted Christ, and been received by him.

In the meantime he had applied himself steadily and faithfully to his business, and not only earned the respect of his employers, but saved a good share of his money.

"And now," he thought, triumphantly, " there is nothing to prevent me from going home."

This thought took complete possession of him, and in his leisure moments he did little else than picture to himself his home-coming, and the sight of mother, sister, and brother. They would rejoice, he was sure, in his new life. He wondered if Flora had changed much, and in what way Alec passed away the days.

These thoughts of home and home-folks, together with the great desire to see them again, gradually wore away the feeling of shame with which he had been assailed whenever his thoughts had turned that way before.

"Joel!" he exclaimed, as they were sitting together, one pleasant evening, " I see no other way but to do it!"

"What is it you mean, my boy?" asked Joel, as he looked at Harry for a moment, and then returned to his book.

"To go home, and see them all," returned Harry.

"Believe I will too," said Joel, slapping his book by way of emphasis. " By the way, Harry," he continued, " my home isn't so very far from yours; only a couple of hours' ride. You live at Bartonville and I live at Brinton, or rather, I did."

"Is that so? Well, then, let us go together."

"What do you intend to do? Give up your situation here for good, or just ask for leave of absence?" asked Joel.

"Oh, I shall give it up entirely," was the answer. "I prefer to get something to do nearer home. What will you do?"

"I shall come back," said Joel, decidedly. "My people are farmers. I could be of no service now on a farm, you know, even if I cared for it, which I don't."

Thus the matter was decided, and arrangements were made accordingly.

One evening, as Mrs. Hazeley sat in her home, all alone, stitching away busily, she was startled to hear a loud rap on the door.

"Who can it be?" she thought, rising to answer the knock. She found herself confronted by a tall, rather slight young man, with a grave face, which, however, was now illuminated by a smile of expectancy.

"Harry! Harry! my boy Harry!" she cried, holding open her arms. The mother's quick instinct and penetrating love could not be deceived by appearances, no matter how altered. The form might be changed, and the features matured, but there was something that brought to her the memory of her child, the baby of long ago.

After the first greetings were over, Harry settled down, and prepared to unburden his mind. His mother noticed that he glanced about him wistfully and inquiringly.

"No," said Mrs. Hazeley, answering the query in his eyes, "Flora is not here. She went to stay with your Aunt Sarah, who is very ill. I am expecting to go myself, whenever I hear from her to that effect. Alec too, is away. He is living with that good old man, 'Major Benson,' you used to call him, you remember. Alec enjoys a country life. He intends to be a farmer, he says. It was very kind of him to give the boy such an opening. The poor child was so afraid of being a burden to us. I have every reason to be grateful for my children."

"Except me, mother," said Harry.

"No, my boy," returned his mother, looking keenly at him. "I am sure I have reason to be grateful for you too. But tell me, Harry, where have you been, and why did you not write to us, and keep us posted?"

The entire absence of reproach or fault finding, and the warm affection with which he was received by his mother, touched the young man very deeply, and with his heart

K

made tender with these thoughts, he determined to confide fully all his past to his mother, from whom he felt sure he would receive ready sympathy.

When the story was told, Mrs. Hazeley could but exclaim, " Bless the Lord, oh my soul ! "

"And forget not all his benefits," added Harry reverently.

They were interrupted at that moment by a knock upon the door—a quick, business-like, energetic knock.

" I know who that is," said Mrs. Hazeley, smilingly, as she arose to admit the new-comer. It was Flora.

" Did ever returned prodigal receive a more hearty welcome than I ? " exclaimed Harry, laughingly, but gratefully.

His old habit of reserve was being gradually overcome, and he was becoming accustomed to express his feelings quite freely, much to the present and subsequent delight of his family.

This evening, a memorable one in the history of the little family, was by no means over. Just as the happy trio were seated, with heads bowed reverently in thankfulness to the Giver of all good, the knocker was raised another time.

As the heads were lifted, and Flora arose to open the door, she remarked, merrily :

"That must be Alec. I suppose the magnetism of our presence is drawing him to us."

It was not Alec. It was our good friend Joel Piper.

"I was told Mrs. Hazeley lived here," said he.

"So she does," answered Flora, trying to recall where she had seen the familiar face before her. Joel was doing the same. He was the first to ask, however, "Haven't I met you before?"

"I was just thinking I had seen you somewhere," said Flora, looking puzzled.

"In Brinton, perhaps?" suggested Joel.

"That is just it—you know—Lottie Piper," exclaimed Flora disconnectedly.

"Yes, yes," said Joel, eagerly; "I'm her brother. I remember now. You are Flora Hazeley. Well, well," he cried, accepting Flora's invitation to enter the room, where he saw his friend Harry, for whom he was hunting. "I was just looking for you, Hal," said he, having first been presented to Mrs. Hazeley, who was delighted to welcome the young man who had done so much for her Harry. "I was looking for you, Hal, but I had no idea I should

meet an old acquaintance, in the shape of your sister. **But**
that reminds me," he added, sadly, " I have been to the
old home. No wonder I didn't hear from them. Sickness,
death, and desolation! I found the home, but no one
in it."

" How could that be?" asked Harry.

" I know," said Flora, gently. " I saw Lottie for a
few moments the other day, and she told me all about it.
I am so sorry."

" Is my sister here?" Joel asked. eagerly.

" Yes, she is here—in Bartonville; she is living with
her aunt."

" I know," said Joel, " my father's sister. I shall be
glad to see Lottie; but mother is gone, and now it is too
late."

" No, no, Joel, don't talk that way," said Harry, soothingly. " You have no need to say that. You haven't
come home as you left it. And suppose your mother
is not here, don't you think she knows all about it?
And then, there is your sister, you know."

" That is all true, Harry. It would have been hard to
have come back as I went away, and found her gone. I
could not have helped the little girl then. But one thing

more," he said, turning to Flora, who was wiping her eyes in sympathy. " Where is my father? "

" Lottie says he went away somewhere, to work."

" Then I shall hope to see him, some day, and that will be one consolation." Joel was comforted by his friends, and his own kind, helpful deeds were bearing fruit for him.

It was arranged that Joel should board—he would hear of no other arrangement—with Mrs. Hazeley until he should find his sister, and see how she was situated, before returning to his employment.

Flora's news was almost forgotten in the general rejoicing over Harry's unexpected return and the equally unexpected addition to the little household in Joel. But when things were somewhat quieted down, she had something wonderful to relate also.

" Well, well, well," said Mrs. Hazeley. " To think of sister Sarah softening, at her age. When will wonders cease ! "

Harry did not approve of this proposed breaking up of their own little home. He feared it might be but a passing whim of Aunt Sarah's.

" Oh, no," maintained Flora, stoutly. " Whatever else

Aunt Sarah is, she is not fickle. When she says she means to do a thing, that thing is as good as done."

" That's very true," said her mother. So it was settled that, after due preparation, the family should move to Brinton.

The only regret that Flora felt at leaving her home in Bartonville was that she would be obliged to part with her class of girls, whom she loved and who loved her. She comforted herself with the thought that she would have another, if possible, in Brinton. The girls she left behind always cherished the memory of their young teacher, and strove to imitate her gentle, earnest ways, and noble traits. Surely, the seed she had sown in their hearts would spring up, blossom, and bear fruit for the Master's kingdom.

CHAPTER XVI.

LOTTIE'S TRIALS.

"WELL! Things have come to a pretty pass! Here I've been running up and down, here and there and everywhere, like a chicken with its head cut off, trying to please Aunt Emmeline, and I'm just about as near doing it now as I was when I commenced. It's grumble, grumble, grumble, every minute in the day; and I will not stand it—not a day longer, now!" and Lottie gave the fire a vigorous shake that sent the sparks darting hither and thither, in every direction.

It was hard for her. Lottie conscientiously did all she could for the fretful invalid upstairs. But her efforts were not appreciated. Instead, Mrs. Durand seemed to grow more irritable daily. Nothing Lottie did pleased her; the tea was either too weak or too strong; the toast either too hot or too cold; the beef-tea was too highly seasoned, or not enough. Thus the fault-finding continued, day in and day out.

Heretofore Lottie had succeeded in bearing with her

captious patient fairly well, her natural patience and
sweetness of disposition being a great help to her. But
this day her task seemed a little harder to bear than
usual, and a short time before the outburst at the opening
of the chapter the climax was reached, when her aunt
struck her with the cane she used to aid her in getting
about the room, for she was able to go about a very little
during the day.

Lottie had been sent for some water, and in her zeal to
please her aunt by being quick about it, had spilled a few
drops in that good woman's lap, and she, without stopping to think, had given her niece a rap with her stick.

"No, I shall not stand it another minute," muttered
Lottie, as she angrily paced the floor of the little room,
whither she had rushed from her aunt's presence.

Apparently she had determined to do something, for
she went to work energetically to put everything to rights.
She put more coal on the fire, and, in fact, did everything
she deemed necessary. Then she stole quietly up to her
room, packed some things in a bundle, and noiselessly
left the house.

Where was she going? She did not know. What was
she going to do? She only knew that she was going far

Hazeley Family.   Page 153.

away from her Aunt Emmeline's, where she had been
insulted. The old poplar solemnly waved its long, bare
arms over her head, as if wishing her " good-bye." She
had a vague idea she would go and find her friend Flora;
she would at least advise her what to do, for, after once
fairly in the street, the fact that she had no home but
the one she was leaving behind, made itself felt very
plainly.

She had not seen Flora since that first day when they
had met accidentally, and she had almost forgotten the
way she had come, for she had been in such a hurry she
gave little heed to anything. She would go as best she
could remember. It seemed to her that she was walking
a great distance, and when at length she came to a small
public square, she sat down upon one of the cold, damp seats,
almost discouraged, and utterly unhappy. No mother,
no home—nothing but misery. The tears were very near
the surface, when she heard her name called at no great
distance.

That was strange, though the voice sounded familiar.
Stranger still, however, was the sight of a young man
making his way rapidly toward her with a shuffling gait,
and leaning upon two canes. Although the face seemed

familiar, Lottie was frightened, and was preparing to run away when her steps were arrested by the strange young man saying, in half-laughing, half-vexed tones :

" Why, Lottie, girl, don't you know your brother Joel ? "

" What ? Not my brother Joel ? " exclaimed Lottie, joyously, yet distrustfully.

" The very same, and yet not the same," replied Joel, sadly, as he remembered how great was the physical change in him, and which was so apparent.

" I was straight and strong when you last saw me, Lottie," he said, looking down at his twisted limbs. " I was straight and strong when I left the old home, and now you see what I am." And he seated himself beside Lottie, who had remained on the bench.

" Oh, Joel, what made you so ?" she cried, in a distressed voice.

" Never mind about that now, little sister. I will tell you all about it some time. But mother——"

" Didn't you know ? She is dead." And Lottie burst into tears, while the half-repressed sobs of the utterly miserable girl, shook her slender frame.

" Yes, I know," answered her brother, softly.

" How did you know ? " asked Lottie, as she raised her

tear-stained face in surprise at his knowledge, when she knew he had been away so long.

"Never mind that, either," returned Joel; "but tell me everything."

Lottie told about the death of their mother, then added:

"Oh, Joel, she so wanted to see you before she died, and now it's too late."

"Yes, too late." The words found an echo in the young man's own breast. He had put it off too long, this home-coming. Hoping and wanting to come back to his home and parents, well able to take care of himself and to help them too, he had waited, and worked, and saved, and now she for whom he so longed was not here to bid him welcome. The thought also came to him that it was well this "too late" came only in the disappointment of earthly hopes. Suppose it meant the loss of his soul as well? Then another thought came, this time full of comfort and peace:

"She will know I am changed, and I shall meet her in heaven."

Then he turned to his sister, feeling that here was a work for him—a legacy left him by his mother.

"Where is father, Lottie?" he asked a moment later, inwardly wondering at her presence here.

"Father? Oh, after mother's death he couldn't stay there any more, he said, and so he went away to work. Out west, I believe," she added, rather glad than otherwise to break the silence that had followed her last words. "I haven't seen him since he brought me to live here."

"Live here? With whom?" inquired her brother.

"With Aunt Emmeline." And then she poured forth into sympathetic ears a recital of her woes, inflicted largely by her aunt.

"What are you going to do?" asked Joel, when she finished. "Are you going back?"

"No, I am not. That settles it!"

"Never?"

"No, never!"

Joel was amused. He well knew that the angry girl would be obliged, sooner or later, to modify her emphatic and hasty assertions. However, he thought it best to make no criticism, at least until she should see her folly and mistake herself; so he only said:

"Well, I guess you had better come with me just now. Both of us will catch cold if we stay here much longer."

Unquestioningly, Lottie arose. She did not care where she went, so long as she was with Joel, who now was all she had to cling to.

The sight of poor, deformed Joel, hobbling painfully along, touched Lottie's heart as nothing else could have done, as she contrasted his shrunken body with her own strong, robust self. She felt almost glad her mother could not see him now—she had been so proud of Joel's strength.

At length they halted before a small house that appeared strangely familiar to Lottie, and Joel rapped on the door. What was her surprise and delight to see the door opened by Flora Hazeley.

" Lottie!" the latter exclaimed.

"Flora!"

Joel stood by, smilingly, while Lottie was introduced to the rest of the family.

" It seems so strange that both your brother and mine should be returned runaways, doesn't it, Flora?" remarked Lottie, when all were seated.

" How about Lottie?" slyly whispered Joel, as he sat by her side.

Lottie deigned no reply, but tossed her head willfully,

while she thought: "No, I will never go back to Aunt Emmeline's."

It was a very pleasant little home party that sat and chatted in the old dining room that evening, but it was not until Lottie and Flora were alone in the room which they were to share for the night, that Lottie opened her heart, and poured out her woes into Flora's sympathetic ear.

"Oh, Lottie, how could you?" asked Flora, when the recital was over.

"Oh, Flora, of course I could do it, and so would you have done, in my place," returned Lottie, in an injured tone.

"Is it possible that you have left your poor, sick aunt all alone?"

"She isn't very sick; she only thinks she is," said Lottie, sulkily. "She can get about her room well enough. It won't hurt her to go a bit farther, and go downstairs."

Flora, after a few more ineffectual words, saw Lottie was feeling too bitter and hurt to be ashamed of her desertion of her poor, sick aunt, and, with her customary tact, dropped the subject entirely. For a few moments there was silence, each busy with her own thoughts.

As Flora was brushing her hair, of which she was justly proud, she said :

"Lottie, let us sit here in front of the fire. I often do, and watch the sparks as they flit here and there. I feel like talking to-night. I have listened to your story. Now, you come here with me ; I want to tell you mine."

Nothing loth, Lottie seated herself, and listened attentively while her friend told of her own life, with all of its disappointments, hardships, and trials.

" What has all this to do with me ? " asked Lottie, suspiciously, for she had a vague idea that Flora had an object in view.

"It has this to do with you, Lottie dear," answered Flora, as she put her own shapely hand, gently but firmly, over the rebellious one in Lottie's lap. " It will show you that none of us can have things exactly as we want them, and we are cowards if we run away from our duties. Had I been left to choose what I wished, I should not have chosen a single thing that came to me, and yet I am sure everything turned out for the very best. In the first place, Aunt Sarah's sending me home made me think and act for myself and others, and in doing so I became far stronger than I would have been had I stayed with, and depended on Aunt Bertha, if she had lived. In doing the second, I found pleasure, and now that after all our worrying Harry has come back so changed, I am just as happy as I can be. But suppose I had run away, when things were dark and discouraging, would I now have anything to be happy over?"

"But nobody ever struck you, Flora. That is different," said Lottie, looking less stubborn.

"No," replied Flora; "that is very true, dear; nobody ever struck me, but I have had other things quite as hard. Indeed, things that I thought I could not possibly endure. But, you know who helped me bear them, don't you, Lottie dear?"

"Yes," was the subdued reply. "You mean God helped you."

"Yes, and he will help you too, Lottie, if you will let him. But you must take up your duties again, you know."

"What? go back to Aunt Emmeline?"

"Yes, I mean just that. I am sure she did not intend to treat you badly. She will tell you so, I have no doubt, some day."

"I don't know about that," said Lottie; "but, I guess

I ought to go. But, suppose she will not have me back again; what then? "

"Oh, don't borrow trouble. It will be time enough to think about that when it happens," replied Flora. "But come, it's time we were asleep."

Sleep, however, did not come to Lottie as soon as it did to her friend. Her mind was too busy, turning over the events of the day, and anticipating the possible ones of the morrow. Nevertheless, Lottie was not really a coward, and when she had decided on a certain course, she kept to it, as we have already seen.

CHAPTER XVII.

MORE SURPRISES.

NEXT day, Lottie informed her brother of her decision to return to her aunt, and apologize for her unceremonious departure.

Joel was very glad that she had come to this conclusion of her own free will, for he had feared he might have trouble in bringing her to it. He more than half-suspected that Flora had a good deal to do with his sister's present submissive state, and was accordingly grateful.

Lottie bade her friends good-bye, and with Joel to keep her courage up, turned her face determinedly toward her aunt's home, only making a comical grimace, as Flora whispered to her some words of encouragement, adding the assurance that all would come out right.

The brother and sister walked on together in silence, for some time; and then it was Joel who talked, for Lottie was too busy thinking to care for conversation. She acted as guide until they stood under the old poplar in front of the quiet little house, and then she took refuge behind her brother, who marched undauntedly up to the door, and gave a knock, which said plainly: "Here are some people who mean business."

The knock evidently surprised Mrs. Durand, for she opened the door herself, instead of telling them to "Come in," as was her usual custom.

At first she saw no one but Joel, and seemed strongly inclined to close the door upon him; but when she caught sight of Lottie, standing demurely behind him, she steadied herself firmly upon her canes, and inquired, "What do you want?"

"In the first place, Aunt Emmeline," said Joel, calmly, "I suppose you know me?"

"No, I can't say I do," was the reply.

"I am not much surprised. It has been some time since we met. I am Joel Piper, your nephew, and Lottie's brother."

Mrs. Durand said nothing, but only stood and looked.

"Lottie, come here; Aunt Emmeline, Lottie has something to say to you."

Lottie came from behind her brother, and speaking rapidly, as if she were afraid she would lose courage if she did not talk fast, said: "I've come to say that I am sorry I acted so badly, Aunt Emmeline, and if you will let me, I'll come back again."

" Come in," was the brusque command. Joel and Lottie entered, and Mrs. Durand closed the door. Then she turned to them, and said, simply :

" If you want to come back, I guess you may."

Lottie shrugged her shoulders. She wanted so much to say that she did not come back because she wanted to, but because she thought she ought, and she bit her tongue, by way of admonishing that unruly member to keep still.

Joel guessed something of what was passing in his sister's mind, and hastened to engage Mrs. Durand in conversation.

She seemed really touched as the young man recounted the history of his sickness and sufferings in a strange city ; and Lottie, sitting silently listening, was more than half convinced that she had judged her aunt too severely. By the time Joel was ready to go, she was quite satisfied that she *did* want to come back. Then the old house really looked homelike, especially after the feeling of loneliness and homesickness she had experienced the day before as she walked the streets not knowing which way to look for shelter.

That evening, after everything was done, as Mrs. Durand was seated by the fire in her easy chair, and Lottie was hemming a table-cloth, Mrs. Durand asked abruptly :

" Why did you come back ? "

Lottie looked up in astonishment, scarcely knowing what to say. But deeming it best to tell her exact reason, she said : " Because I thought it was my duty to do it."

For a while there was silence, during which Lottie glanced up timidly to see the effect of her words upon her aunt, but she could discover nothing.

" I suppose you were pretty angry with me, when you went ? " was the next remark.

" Awful ! " said Lottie, catching her breath at her own temerity.

Again there was silence.

" Well," returned Mrs. Durand, " if you hadn't been in such a hurry, I should have told you I didn't mean to strike you ; but, I suppose I can tell you so now, can't I ? "

" Oh dear, Aunt Emmeline, you needn't say anything at all about it," said Lottie, eagerly. " I acted just horrid ; I know I did."

" I can't blame you much, child. Old people like me, with the rheumatism, are apt to be snappish. But I guess

we both have had a lesson we will not be likely to forget.
Come, now, I think it is time you were in bed, so put
away your sewing, and go."

"Can I get you anything, aunt?" asked Lottie, as she
prepared to obey.

"Nothing at all, my dear," was the soft reply, that sent
Lottie upstairs in a state of pleasurable surprise at the
turn things had taken. Never had she felt more glad of
anything than she was to find herself in the little chamber
again, because it was home.

Joel, in the meantime, after he had seen his sister fairly
reinstated in her old place, returned to Mrs. Hazeley's,
where he duly reported the success of his visit.

Flora was very glad things were straightening out for
her young friend, Lottie, for she was really fond of her,
because of her open, truthful nature.

A few days more Joel spent with his friends, and then,
after arranging with his aunt for his sister's future, insisting on supplying her needs outside of her board, for which
Mrs. Durand would accept nothing, he left, to return to
his work, feeling at least contented, if not carrying back
with him the memory of a happy home welcome and
reunion. It was good to have somebody to work for and

care for, and Joel was accustomed to placing full value upon present blessings or privileges, and his example had not been lost upon Lottie, whose lot, while greatly changed and improved, was by no means entirely freed from thorns, for Aunt Emmeline was still Aunt Emmeline, and was likely to continue to be so. However, since Lottie's return, she had treated the girl with a fair amount of consideration, much to her satisfaction and enjoyment. Lottie was beginning to feel at home. In fact, as the months rolled by, and she grew in age and experience, Lottie gradually became the household manager, and her aunt was content to oversee.

After a time, Mr. Piper grew tired of " rolling around," as he informed his sister and daughter, and determined to marry a second time. He moreover informed Lottie that it would be more agreeable to all concerned if she would conclude to remain with her aunt.

" Humph ! " said that good woman. " It's well that it is agreeable to all ; but suppose it wasn't ? As it is, child," she added, " you know you are welcome to a home with me just as long as you want it. I have no wish to part with you. But I must say, your father is pretty cool."

At one time Lottie's heart would have beaten tumult-

uously at the prospect of a permanent home with Aunt
Emmeline, but it was not so now, and she felt very grateful, when she lay down that night, that God had so cared
for her, when she could not care for herself.

To return to our friends, the Hazeleys. They had all
removed to Brinton, all but Alec, who seemed so well-con-
tented with his quarters at Major Joe's, that he did not
wish to change. There was really no necessity for him
to do so. He was doing well at school, although he was
by no means what might be considered a brilliant pupil.
In fact, his own prediction that he would be no scholar,
but a practical farmer, seemed likely to come true.

Major Joe had other help now, and Alec gave his time
out of school and during holidays, to the owner of a large
farm in the immediate neighborhood, where he was learning many things that were needful to know in his chosen
calling. He always came home at night, and was known all
around as a "fine lad." Major Joe had grown too feeble
to attend market any longer, and so he had turned that
part of his business over to the young man, who now had
charge of his garden, and who, it seemed more than likely
would have charge of Ruth some time in the future, when
he had grown able to do so. The major remained at

home, alternately nursing his rheumatic limbs, and helping "mother" and Ruth with the poultry, of which they raised a quantity, and, as Jem said, were "getting awful rich off the eggs and things." Ruth was a thrifty, thorough-going little housekeeper, one after her grandmother's own heart, while Jem was just a lively little girl, who insisted on bestowing her help, which, however, usually proved more of a hindrance. She was, however, the pet of the old people, and made things merry in the little cottage.

Alec Hazeley had gone to see his brother as soon as he had heard of his return, and had spent some days at home prior to the removal of the family. And he was the last object they saw as they steamed out of the station. Mrs. Martin was no longer the active, stirring woman she had been before her illness, but was now a confirmed invalid. She was much altered, in every way, and was very glad to have her sister and family with her; and they were altogether a peaceful, happy, little household.

It was not Harry's intention to remain at home long after he had seen his mother and sister settled. But, somehow—perhaps it was because every one seemed glad to have him there—he stayed longer than he had intended; and, surprising to himself, and altogether delightful to

Flora and his mother, he one day informed them that he felt he had received a decided call to the ministry.

"Oh, Harry!" cried his sister. "How sudden! I wasn't dreaming of such a thing; but I am *so* glad."

"Yes," answered Harry, seriously, "I feel as if I must prepare myself to preach. Something tells me, and I feel sure it is the voice of God, that I shall prosper at nothing else but winning souls for Christ. As I was snatched from the toils of the Evil One, so must I help save others. I believe that God rescued me for that very purpose."

Aunt Sarah was delighted, and would hear of nothing but that he should immediately begin to fit himself for his new work. The family circle was again broken, but this time, how different the circumstances, and how hopeful the future appeared, with all united in the bond of love for Christ and a hope for his re-appearing.

CHAPTER XVIII.

A CHRISTMAS INVITATION

YEARS have passed, and long since the grass was green over Mrs. Martin's grave. Side by side she lay with her gentle sister, and over the two graves the graceful branches of the willow drooped, and in summer the sod was starred with daisies.

It was December. The trees were bare of leaves, and the grass was withered. The weather was cold. The folks in Brinton predicted a hard winter. In the cosy home where Mrs. Hazeley now presided with a calm demeanor, and Flora flitted about happy and contented, there seemed no need to fear the searching winds of winter. Flora was no longer a girl, but a well-grown young woman—changed, and yet not changed. She had matured with years; but it was easy to discern the same merry, thoughtful Flora of the old days.

Shortly after his conversion, Harry had heard and followed the voice of his Master to "preach the gospel," and now he was the pastor of the church where Aunt

Bertha had sat and listened to the gospel, eagerly taking in the blessed words of life—the same church where Aunt Sarah had listened, stern and cold, with her hard features turned upward to the minister; and the same church where two happy faces—one of a quiet and attractive-looking matron: the other of a fair, bright-eyed younger woman—were seen every Lord's Day.

Very proud was Flora of her manly, earnest brother who had won so completely the hearts of the people ; and equally proud was Harry of his sister, who was loved and respected by all.   They saw but little of Alec, who had never outgrown his love for the country, and who still lived in Brinton.   He was industrious and economical, and his friends were sure he would some day be a wealthy man.

It wanted but a few days to Christmas, when, one after-noon, during a few idle moments, Flora stood by the window lightly drumming against the pane, and smiling, as if her thoughts were very pleasant.

 She had not been standing there long when the front gate opened, and Harry came toward the house.

Flora hurried to open the door for him, and pausing to remove his overcoat, he said :

"Here is a letter for you, Flo."

"A letter for me?" she repeated. "I wonder from whom it can be." She returned to the room with the letter in her hand.

"A letter, Flora?" inquired her mother. "Who is writing to you, dear?"

"It is from Alec, mother," was the answer, a moment later.

"What does the dear boy say—anything of importance?" asked Mrs. Hazeley.

"It is a very short letter. Shall I read it?"

"Never mind, Flora; just tell us what he wants."

"It is simply a very short, but very urgent, invitation for us all to spend Christmas with him. You, especially, Harry."

"Me? I wonder why?"

"Shall we go, mother?"

"Of course. I would not disappoint the boy for anything; besides, we have not seen him for so long."

All were satisfied with this arrangement.

Christmas morning dawned bright and clear, but very cold.

Harry held service in the morning in his church, and

of course Mrs. Hazeley and Flora were present. Everything was in readiness to start away immediately at its
close.

"It will not really matter; and we cannot miss seeing
our Harry conduct his first Christmas service," said Flora,
positively.

The exercises were simple but impressive; the singing
sweet and solemn—the sermon earnest and tender. It
seemed to Flora as if she were shut in from everything,
and that she really moved among the circumstances connected with the Saviour's birth. It seemed to her that
she was with the wise men who brought gifts, and came to
worship the infant Jesus; and the words of the anthem,
"Glory to God in the highest, peace on earth, good will
to men," echoed and re-echoed through her whole being.
"Truly," she thought, "that peace has entered my soul,
and how can I have aught but 'good will to men'?"

Mrs. Hazeley's feelings found expression by the tears
rolling down her cheeks under her veil. Flora saw them,
but knew they were for joy.

Never had Harry spoken as he spoke that morning.
He scarcely recognized himself in the preacher whose im-
passioned words were holding spell-bound the people

who filled the church, drawing from them alternately tears of sympathy and smiles of joy.

When the service was at an end, and the usual interchange of Christmas wishes over, the young minister joined his mother and sister, who were waiting for him, and, with one upon each arm, directed his steps to the depot, where they boarded the cars for Alec's home.

Flora felt too peaceful and happy to talk, and, in fact, they were all disinclined for conversation, and so the short journey was made in silence. True to his word, Alec was at the station to welcome them, and delighted that they had all come.

He conducted them to a carriage he had in waiting, and helped them in.

"What do you want to ride to Major Joe's for?" asked Harry. "It is such a short distance."

"Oh, I want you to ride to-day, so ask no more questions," was the saucy reply.

"Alec has some new project in his head," whispered Flora to her mother, who nodded and smiled, as if anything and everything were in order, so far as she was concerned.

Harry asked no more questions, but was busy looking about him, and trying to decide where they were going;

if to Major Joe's, why take such a roundabout course?
All to no avail, however, and he abandoned the matter
to the driver.

There was no snow, to cover with its white, glittering
blanket, the rough spots, but the brightness of the sun
made amends for this lack by gilding the bare places. It
was a green Christmas, but there was a lurking promise
of snows and storms yet to come, in the brisk, sharp wind,
that drove the withered leaves—reminders of the summer's
beauty—along, as Flora remarked, " like little, old women
dressed in brown, and caught in a wind-storm." Alec
noticed, as they drove along, that his brother still glanced
about inquiringly, evidently not yet satisfied as to the
road to Major Joe's from the station. Alec was amused.
It was so long since Harry had been there, he felt sure he
could not remember. It was with a view to drawing his
attention from this, and thus prevent his asking more
questions, that Alec began to talk diligently. He pointed
out the different objects of interest along the way, and then
would branch off into a series of remarks or conjectures
concerning them.

" This now," he said, pointing to a pretty house they
were passing, " is Mrs. Brown's new residence. Isn't it

tasteful? Contains all the latest modern improvements— at least, so they say. And here is the homestead of a well-to-do widow. Very benevolent. Quite a good thing for widows." He was interrupted by Flora's inquiry:

" Why widows especially? "

" Oh, because, you see, all they need is to have just enough to keep them comfortably while they live. They don't care about making improvements, and buying or speculating as a general thing, like——"

" Like what? " asked Harry, drily, as his brother paused.

" Well, like me, for instance," returned Alec.

" So, I suppose you think there is no necessity for you to be benevolent."

" It's not but that I should, so much as I cannot afford to be. You see, I am a young man, and I need to be very prudent about the way I invest what money I have, in order to accumulate a little more."

" Oh, Alec," laughed Flora, " you certainly have accumulated a pretty good stock of self-complacency, and have cultivated a fine opinion of yourself."

" Yes," returned Alec, good-humoredly, touching up

M

his horse with the end of his whip. " One must blow his own trumpet, if no one else will for him."

" Bad policy, my boy," interposed Harry, who seemed for the time being, to feel himself a boy again. " Bad policy. It is better not to have a trumpet blown at all, than to do it yourself. True worth will always receive its proper recognition."

" Not always ; you are wrong there," said Alec, his eyes twinkling mischievously at the success of his plan for diverting his brother's attention.

" Yes, always," persisted Harry. " Probably not from the direction you desire, or are looking toward ; but, if one looks in the right direction, he will find that if he is worthy of esteem, honor, and respect, he will get it from those upon whom his course has made an impression. The trouble is, that people often look too far away. Either they do not think to look among those immediately about them, and among whom they live, or they do not place the proper value upon their opinions and respect."

" Well, well," said Alec, coolly, as he drew up before the gate of a new and very pretty cottage. " I am very much obliged to you for your valuable homily. I hope I shall profit by it. But, my dear brother, ' all is well that ends well'; and as my chief object in engaging you in conversation was to give you something to think about besides which way we were going, I am delighted that I was successful." And with a polite bow, the saucy fellow jumped down and proceeded to help his passengers to alight.

CHAPTER XIX.

A HOMELY WEDDING.

NO sooner had the little party alighted, than the cottage door flew open, and a crowd of familiar faces met their astonished gaze.

There was the old major, wrinkled and lame, leaning on his cane, but smiling as if he had forgotten that there was any "rheumatiz" in the world.

There was the bright-faced little Jem of long ago, now grown into a stout maiden, and looking as sober and matter-of-fact as ever.

And motherly little Ruth was there, with her face wreathed in smiles.

There was good Mrs. Benson, busy and bustling with the weight of some unusual responsibility.

Such a royal welcome as our friends received. Tongues were kept busy with stories of the generosity of the dear old Saint Nicholas, and wishes for the new year.

"What a pretty house!" exclaimed Flora, as the hum of voices was lessening.

"I am glad you like it, sister mine," returned Alec who was at her side, "because, you know, it belongs to me."

"To you? Then you have been industrious in all these years. Are you going to live here all alone?"

"Yes, you are right there, Flora," Alec answered, totally ignoring her question. "I have worked hard, and saved too. But, there! I am blowing my own trumpet again, in spite of Hal's lecture!" And he glanced roguishly at his brother.

But Harry only smiled

"What on earth do you want with a whole house?" asked Flora, curiously. "Are the major and Mrs. Benson going to live with you?" she added, wishing to understand it all.

"No," said Alec, "they are going back home."

Flora and Harry were thoroughly puzzled, and from time to time glanced at their brother questioningly, as if they feared he was joking them. Flora noticed, however, what the others were all too busy to see, that Alec was constantly glancing out of the front window, as if expecting some one.

At last her curiosity and his evident uneasiness were both satisfied; for a buggy drove up to the door, and from

it alighted a young girl and an elderly woman, and—
Joel Piper, who after dismissing the conveyance came
toward the house, where they were met by Alec, who presented them triumphantly to the rest.

"Lottie Piper, is this you?" cried Flora.

The young girl was really Lottie, and the elderly
woman was Mrs. Emmeline Durand, her aunt.

"Yes, it's me," answered Lottie, serenely and ungram-
matically.

"This is a delightful surprise. What next?" exclaimed Flora.

"Shall I tell you?" asked Alec, coming forward and
offering Lottie his arm, who evidently understood the
whole situation; "it is simply this,"—and the two fine-
looking young people walked toward the window where
Harry was standing, and paused before him,—"I love
Lottie, and I think she loves me." Lottie's bright eyes
dropped to the floor, her face suffused with blushes, with a
bright little smile trembling around her mouth. "I love
Lottie; and, Harry, I want you to pronounce us husband
and wife."

Mrs. Hazeley and Flora looked somewhat dazed, and
then, turning to each other, locked arms and walked

toward the bridal pair, each face showing surprise, but also betraying real joy at the event.

The others were happy. All knew what the day would bring forth, and each had united with the others in mystifying Mrs. Hazeley, Flora, and Harry.

The last named, while much surprised, as was but natural, understood the situation and the part he was expected to take, as Alec and Lottie stepped toward him.

"Very well, Alec. I am glad you have made such a happy choice. Are you both ready? Please stand here. That is it. So."

Then, amid the hush that fell upon the little company, Harry's voice was clearly heard, saying:

"'What God hath joined together, let no man put asunder.'"

At the close of the short, but very impressive service, Harry offered a short prayer that the "great All-Father would watch over, guard, and guide these two lives that had linked themselves together for all time."

Then came congratulations, and everybody tried to talk at once. Then came dinner. This was in charge of Mrs. Benson, and it is only necessary to say that it was one long to be remembered; for she was an excellent cook.

In the course of the dinner, Alec was pressed by Flora to tell how he had become acquainted with Lottie. He quite willingly complied.

"I first met her on the day I came down to see you off on the cars when you all left for Brinton; and just as the train was disappearing around a curve, and I was turning about to go home, a girl came running up all out of breath.

"'Oh,' said she, 'has the train gone?' I said, 'Yes; did you want to get on?'

"'No,' said she; 'but my friend is on it, and I wanted to say Good-bye.' 'I'm sorry,' said I, 'but who is your friend?' Not that it was any of my business to know, but somehow or other I felt interested, and she didn't seem to mind, but said: 'Flora Hazeley.' 'That's my sister,' said I; 'do you know her?' 'I guess I do,' was the answer. 'It is too bad; but it can't be helped, I suppose. I'm always late when I should be early, and early when I should be late.'

"This sounded so odd that we both laughed, and then she turned and was out of sight in a very few seconds. I didn't see her again until one day several years afterward, when I was doing business for myself—taking my

Hazeley Family.   Page 184.

vegetables and things to town to sell, you know. It happened on this morning I had some fine, fresh vegetables left over from market, and I wanted to sell them before going home. I went through several streets, knocking at the doors and asking if the folks would like to buy what I had. At one of the houses I met Lottie again. She did not recognize me at first, but amused me very much by the close bargains she drove. 'Well,' said I, 'you are a case.' She looked up at me suddenly, as if she would like to give me a bit of her mind, and she saw who I was. Then, of course, she began to ask after you all; and that is the way we became acquainted. I always went there afterward when I had anything left over, and, when I saw what a close bargain she could drive, and what a good housekeeper she made for her aunt, I thought: 'Lottie is the girl to help a fellow get on in the world.' So, after a while, with the consent of the good aunt and no objections from our brother Joel here, to whom we wrote about the matter, and who came on to see us and give us his blessing, we made the arrangements that you see have been carried out to-day."

"How about Lottie's father?" said Flora, slyly.

"We wrote to him too, and he didn't object, either—

that is, he didn't answer—and silence is consent, you know."

"Alec," said Harry, gravely, "I am glad, of course, to see you doing well; but it hurts me to hear you talk so much about getting rich and saying nothing about higher and better things. What is to become of you when you are called to lay aside the possessions you are striving so hard to get?"

"Now, never you mind Alec, my good preacher brother," interposed Lottie, looking at him with a complacent smile. "Alec is fond of mystifying people. He is just as good a Christian as ever a young man was. He and I both—to set your mind at rest—were converted over a year ago, at a revival in Bartonville. We mean to try and live right—don't we, Alec?" And she beamed on everybody, in no way abashed by her frank confession. It was plain that Lottie would be matter-of-fact and practical to the end of her days.

"My dear Alec, give me your hand!" cried Harry. And the two brothers clasped hands warmly, while Joel nodded approvingly. Flora, who sat next to Lottie, slipped her arm around her waist and gave her a sisterly embrace; and Mrs. Hazeley exclaimed, wiping the tears away: "If ever a woman was blessed in her children, I am that one. Truly, God is good."

"That he is," rejoined Mrs. Benson. "My husband and I can testify to that." And her eyes rested lovingly upon Ruth and little Jem.

"Well," put in Mrs. Durand, Lottie's aunt. "*You* are all rejoicing; but I am not so sure that I can join you. I lose my housekeeper and the only companion I have when I lose Lottie. One doesn't mind living alone so much when one is used to it; but when you have had company for so long, it comes awkward to go back to the old habits."

"Remember the old proverb, Aunt Emmeline, 'Never cross the bridge until you come to it,'" laughed Lottie. Then, turning to Alec, who sat quietly smiling, she said: "Tell her, Alec, do."

"Aunt Emmeline, come with me a moment; I have something to show you," and offering her his arm they left the room. Crossing the wide hall, they ascended the stairs, and stopping at a closed door, Alec said, as he pushed it open:

"This room is for Aunt Emmeline, as long as she will occupy it. We could not do without her."

Mrs. Durand's fears were thrown to the wind when she heard this, and saw the dainty room. Turning to Alec, with her eyes bright with tears, she said, as she threw her arms around his neck:

"Oh, Alec, I do not deserve this. But it makes me very happy to know you think enough of me to do this for me."

As they entered the room, where all was gayety, her face wreathed in smiles, Mrs. Durand said:

"Now I can join in the general rejoicing. I have a new home--this one—with Lottie and Alec."

Everybody was pleased, and Lottie looked her happiness; for her face was ever very expressive of her feelings.

For a long time Jem, who was as quiet and quaint in her ways as ever, had been occupied in the effort to make peace between Dolby and Pokey, who were now old and feeble, but very dear to the heart of their mistress, who had insisted that they must come to the wedding.

During Alec's story, Flora had caught a look of decided disapproval on Jem's face, and determining to ascertain the cause, she asked:

"Jem, dear, does anything trouble you? What do you think of this?"

"Do you mean the wedding?" Jem questioned.

"Yes."

"Well, then,"—and the words came slowly, distinctly, and decisively,—"I think it was a very disinteresting one."

"How would you have had things, if you could have had your way?" asked Flora, much amused at Jem's positive tone.

"Oh, *I'd* have had white satin, and orange blossoms, and lots of presents, and a great big wedding cake, with a beautiful ornament on top, and all such, you know." In her earnestness she had forgotten that Pokey was on her lap, hidden under the table-cloth, for fear her indulgent grandma would see her and be disgusted, and banish her from the room. Pokey, feeling that the little hands were no longer pressing her down and reminding her that she must lie still, quietly dropped to the floor, and began cautiously to explore.

"Now, Jem," went on Flora, argumentatively, "suppose we did have all the fine things you named, how much happier would that make us all?"

"Oh, I don't know anything about that. I only know it would have been prettier, and more to my taste as a guest, you see," returned Jem with dignity, much to the amusement of her listeners.

"Ah, Jem," said Harry, shaking his head at her, and pretending to be very serious: "Ah, Jem, you little know how much unhappiness often follows the orange blossoms and satin."

"I don't know anything about that, either," was the cool rejoinder. "I only know they are prettier to look at."

"Everybody to his taste, say I, Jem," remarked Alec, solemnly; which bit of philosophy was promptly put into practice by Dolby, who evidently found it to his taste just then to spring upon Pokey while her young mistress was busy talking, and who received a sharp box on the ear for his pains. Of course such behavior necessitated the removal of poor Pokey in disgrace by Jem.

Before anybody was ready for it, the hour of separation had come. After a great deal of talking and a good many "good-byes," the Hazeleys were on the cars, being carried back to Brinton, and the unique reunion was over.

"What a queer Christmas party we have been to!" laughed Flora, when they were again at home. "But I enjoyed it."

"Yes," answered Harry. "So did I."

"And I," added his mother, "more than all. Just to think, what wonderful things God does bring about!"

"Yes," said Harry, reverently, "how well the words of Isaiah apply to us: 'I will lead them in paths that they have not known. I will make darkness light before them, and crooked things straight.'"

THE END.